Celebrations 101

Also by Rick Rodgers

Best Barbecues Ever with Irena Chalmers (Longmeadow, 1990)

Best-Ever Brownies with Joan Steuer (Contemporary, 1990)

The Turkey Cookbook (HarperCollins, 1990)

365 Ways to Cook Hamburger and Other Ground Meats (HarperCollins, 1991)

Best-Ever Chocolate Desserts (Contemporary, 1992)

The Slow Cooker Ready and Waiting Cookbook (Morrow, 1992)

Mr. Pasta's Healthy Pasta Cookbook (Morrow, 1994)

Mississippi Memories with The Delta Queen Steamboat Co. (Morrow, 1994)

The Perfect Parties Series: Picnics and Tailgate Parties; Bridal and Baby Showers; Romantic Dinners and Breakfasts; Birthday Celebrations (Warner, 1996)

On Rice: 60 Toppings that Make the Meal (Chronicle Books, 1997)

50 Best Stuffings and Dressings (Broadway Books, 1997)

Fondue: Fabulous Food to Dip, Dunk, Savor, and Swirl (Morrow, 1998)

Simply Shrimp (Chronicle Books, 1998)

Thanksgiving 101 (Broadway Books, 1998)

Fried and True (Chronicle Books, 1999)

Christmas 101 (Broadway Books, 1999)

Pressure Cooking for Everyone (Chronicle Books, 2000)

Williams-Sonoma: Chicken with Chuck Williams (Time-Life, 2001)

Barbecues 101 (Broadway Books, 2001)

Kaffeehaus: Exquisite Desserts from the Classic Cafés of Vienna, Budapest, and Prague (Clarkson Potter, 2002)

Dip It! (Morrow, 2002)

The Carefree Cook (Broadway Books, 2003)

Celebrations 101

RICK RODGERS

Broadway Books

New York

PRINTED IN CHINA

BROADWAY BOOKS and its logo, a letter B bisected on the diagonal, are trademarks of Random House, Inc.

Visit our website at www.broadwaybooks.com

First edition published 2004

Book design by Ph.D., www.phdla.com, adapted from *The Carefree Cook*
Photography by Mark Ferri

Library of Congress Cataloging-in-Publication Data
Rodgers, Rick, 1953–
    Celebrations 101 / Rick Rodgers.
      p. cm.
    Includes index.
    1. Cookery. I. Title.

TX714.R615 2004

641.5–dc22

2003065524

ISBN 0-7679-1464-3

10 9 8 7 6 5 4 3 2 1

Acknowledgments

At Broadway Books: Publisher Steve Rubin; director of marketing Jackie Everly-Warren; my editor, Jennifer Josephy, and her assistant, Allyson Giard; publicist Jessica Silcox; art director John Fontana; copy editor Sonia Greenbaum; and proof-reader Valerie Saint-Rossy.

At Mark Ferri Photography: Photographer Mark Ferri; food stylist A. J. Battifarano; her assistant, Amy Marcus; and prop stylist Fran Matalon-Degni.

At Writers House: My agent/dear friend, Susan Ginsburg, and her assistant, Rachel Spector.

At home: My hardworking assistant, Diane Kniss; our cohort Steve Evasew; and my partner and party co-host, Patrick Fisher. My parents, Dick and Eleanor Rodgers, for their constant inspiration. Thanks to David Bonom, Skip Dye, David Lebovitz, Chris Styler, Jean Turpen, and Kelly Volpe for sharing recipes.

Contents

Introduction

Even the best home cooks can be challenged by cooking an entire holiday meal. Festive occasions almost always have a crowd of people around the table and require multiple courses of traditional foods, putting unwelcome pressure on the cook. In three books, *Thanksgiving 101*, *Christmas 101*, and *Barbecues 101*, I shared what I had learned from the countless parties I've served up as a home cook, cooking teacher, and caterer. Now, the tradition continues with *Celebrations 101*.

A recent survey showed that Americans go to about twenty-four parties a year, proving that there are many opportunities to celebrate life, family, and friendship with a great meal. The most obvious occasions for celebrations are the holidays that punctuate the year, and you'll find complete menus for these special days in this book. Often these same menus can also be pressed into service for graduations, anniversaries, birthdays, promotions and retirements, wedding and baby showers, baptisms and communions, small-scale bar and bat mitzvahs, and more.

Cooking is always personal. Whenever I plan a menu for a party, I am influenced by my memories of past celebrations, my travels (especially to the Mediterranean and Vienna), restaurant meals, recipes from friends, cookbooks and food magazines, the present season, traditional holiday foods, the amount of time I have to prepare the meal, my budget, the likes and dislikes of the guests, the availability of ingredients, and more. That's a lot to digest. But using these different components will guide you to a successful party.

I come from a family of party lovers. When I was growing up, hardly a weekend went by when there wasn't a birthday party for someone in our family or at a neighbor's, or a month that didn't feature a family holiday dinner. If you think I'm exaggerating, do the math. My great-grandmother had eight children who lived in the area, and my grandmother had seven children. That is a lot of aunts and uncles, great-aunts and great-uncles, cousins and second cousins.

Our stretch of California tract houses on Bockman Road was famous for its parties. Actually, we were infamous. My mother very recently admitted to me how one day she was accosted at a parent-teacher's meeting by a curious neighbor from another block.

"You sure have a lot of parties over there. Makes you kind of wonder what's going on," she smirked. When my mother pressed for specifics, it seemed that some jealous folks suspected our innocently fun-loving block of everything from wife-swapping to the manufacture of bootleg Thunderbird (the grown-ups' wine of choice at that time). My mother was rightfully indignant, and after telling the woman off, never spoke to her again. Much, much worse, that neighbor was never invited to any of our parties!

Party giving was a very important social skill that my parents passed down to me. Even though the food at our parties was always delicious, I learned that a gathering wasn't just about the food—it was also about being with your guests. If the cook is hassled or hurried, this takes time away from visiting, not to mention the wear and tear on body and mind.

There are a few reasons my parents could give a party so easily. The first is that they used recipes that they were familiar with and everyone loved. Mom had reliable recipes for tample pie, lasagna, and ham that she could do in her sleep, recipes that were usually made ahead and popped in the oven before the guests arrived. Also, Mom and Dad divided chores and worked together over a few days—there was little last-minute fussing. Because they entertained often, they had a plentiful supply of plates, glasses, silverware, and a large coffee urn. They had the right utensils for the job, including a couple of huge skillets that could easily handle lots of ingredients. When the biggest skillet wasn't sufficient, Mom would place her turkey roaster over two burners, and use that as a supersized skillet.

I am sure that I became a food professional because of my family's example of carefree entertaining. It was a natural extension for me to become a caterer. When planning other people's parties, I learned early on that time was money. So, I developed recipes that looked and tasted great, but didn't require mountains of time. And many of those recipes are in this book. I also discovered that the key to a successful party is in the planning. A well-organized shopping list and preparation timetable could make the difference between a carefree party and a nightmarish one. Therefore, each menu comes with a shopping list and a timetable, if you choose to prepare the entire menu as given.

One of my favorite distillations of simplified entertaining comes from an unlikely source: André Simon, a gourmand of the highest order. One would think that a professional gourmet (Simon was one of the most influential French food writers of the mid-twentieth century) would advise serving truffles, caviar, and fine wines. Instead, Simon said, "The best host is not he who spends the most money to entertain his guests, but he who takes the most intelligent interest in their welfare and makes sure that they will have a good time (and) something good to drink. . . ." That is *Celebrations 101* in a nutshell.

Carefree Entertaining

I am often asked by food magazines to create complete holiday meals. These articles are always extremely popular because an entire menu, especially with a shopping list and a preparation timetable, is an immeasurable help in organizing and executing any party. The day after the holiday, my e-mailbox is full of messages like, "Your menu saved my life because all I had to do was follow the instructions." So while I encourage you to personalize your party menus, I also know the advantages of having a blueprint. Therefore, each menu in this book also includes a shopping list and timetable.

I am a practical cook, so I have tried not to use too many hard-to-find ingredients. I have also kept a "multigenerational palate" in mind, and attempted to create recipes that everyone in the family will enjoy. Again, feel free to substitute a favorite fam-

Celebration Central

Here are a few basic tips to help keep your party under control.

Make lists I've already provided you with a grocery list and a preparation timetable for each menu. I create a list of necessary utensils and serving dishes (in doing so, I often find a missing utensil or two), and a tableware list (which helps me avoid discovering that I am short on dessert forks at the last minute). Write up the menu with all incidentals (like coffee, tea, cream and sugar, and butter for bread) and tack it up in your kitchen to remind you of little details that could fall through the cracks.

Make a table map If you are serving a buffet, lay out all of the serving dishes on the table to be sure that everything fits—you may have to pull a sideboard or card table into play. Be sure that you have enough serving utensils, too.

Make room for your guests Recently, we hosted a buffet dinner for thirty people at our house. Knowing that our furniture would crowd the guests, we rearranged everything and even moved a few pieces into the garage for temporary storage. If you have a space problem, be ruthless with your furniture rearrangement—if that big side chair can be replaced by three folding chairs, move the big chair elsewhere.

Make time for yourself It's easy to feel rushed even at the most organized party. Choose what you are going to wear well ahead of the event, and be sure that it is ironed and ready to go. This way, if you can barely find time to shower before the guests arrive, at least you won't have to deal with your wardrobe at the last minute, too.

---

ily cake for the recommended dessert or make another recipe swap in a menu. If you change a recipe, please remember to change the shopping list and prep list, too.

When developing recipes, I considered the size of an average kitchen, and assumed that the cook will only have one oven with two racks. If you have two ovens, so much the better. The recipes were designed to fit into average baking dishes, usually 15 × 10 inches (4 quarts) or 13 × 9 inches (3 quarts). You can substitute oval or round baking dishes with the same capacity, if you wish.

Most recipes serve eight to twelve guests, twelve being the maximum number that most people can deal with, simply in terms of tableware if nothing else. However, the recipes are easily multiplied to make more servings. For example, each recipe in the Halloween party menu makes about ten servings. If you are inviting thirty guests, you can triple the recipes without worry.

One word of warning about multiplying recipes for baked goods: Trying to multiply them indefinitely could lead to unhappy results. This is a fact of life, and not just a quirk of these recipes. Luckily, you can usually double the ingredients to a dessert without trouble. However, divide the batter between two pans of the required size instead of using one larger pan.

I do not provide an appetizer for every menu because the Holiday Cocktail Party is filled with hors d'oeuvres. Choose one or two appropriate to the menu, add the ingredients to the shopping list and the recipe preparation to the timetable, and you're done. And you may notice that I don't offer roast- or grilled-beef recipes that would be best served rare or medium-rare. The main reason for this is that it is often difficult for all the guests to agree on the doneness of the beef, and well-done braised beef (such as chili or brisket) deliciously serves a crowd with ease.

As for beverages, some menus have special drinks, but I stayed away from detailed wine suggestions. While it is sometimes good to know that a specific vintage wine goes perfectly with a menu, it can also unduly threaten the host or hostess, who may feel that their party will be compromised if they don't serve that very wine. Also, I'd rather not impose a budget one way or the other.

Each shopping list shows the ingredients for a single batch of each recipe in the menu. Ingredients are alphabetized within categories that seemed the most practical, such as meats, produce, dairy, and groceries (generally nonperishables). If I had a floor plan for every grocery store in America, I would have been tempted to organize the ingredients according to their specific aisles in the markets! Staples such as sugar and flour have the required amount for that menu—there's no need to go out and buy a 5-pound sack of something if a recipe uses ¼ cup and you still have a few cups in the pantry. Also, I have given the measured amount required for most groceries, as it doesn't take much effort to determine what size jar of pimiento-stuffed olives to buy to make ½ cup chopped olives, but there is a certain tyranny in asking you to buy 2½ ounces of such olives from a delicatessen. As the vast majority of kitchens already have salt and pepper, I have not included them in the shopping lists.

The Party Pantry

It's impossible to throw a carefree party without the right utensils. If you only have one 9-inch skillet, don't expect to enjoy cooking for a crowd. You don't need to have an entire catering setup, just a few utensils and appliances in addition to a reasonably well-stocked kitchen. These are the tools that I have used most often in this book.

Large pot Essential for cooking large amounts of vegetables and pasta, this pot should have a minimum capacity of 7 quarts. One pot of this size will be sufficient for most kitchens.

Large skillets Don't try to crowd ingredients into a too small skillet. Have at least one 12-inch skillet with a lid for sautéing vegetables, browning meats, and other chores. Heavy-gauge skillets give the best results. A nonstick surface is more versatile for cooking fish and other delicate foods, but regular uncoated surfaces work well, too. The best-equipped kitchens have one of each.

Large bowls When making potato salad for twenty, you'll be glad that you had a really wide, deep bowl or two.

Dutch oven This heavy-bottomed pot should be attractive enough to be used for serving as well as cooking. My 8-quart Le Creuset, made of enameled cast iron, gets a workout in my kitchen.

V-slicer This handy slicing utensil is much less expensive than a mandoline, but just as efficient. I use mine more often than my food processor because you can get a neater result with the V-slicer (and the processor is usually busy with other jobs).

Baking dishes If you entertain a lot, good-looking baking dishes are a must. Ceramic or glass dishes are the most versatile. If you use glass baking dishes, reduce the oven temperature by 25°F. The most useful sizes are 15 × 10 inches and 13 × 9 inches.

Food processor This appliance changed the way America cooks. I save it for jobs that really can't be done as easily by hand, such as shredding vegetables for slaw.

Blender The food processor did not replace the blender. The latter is still best for puréeing liquid foods and other jobs (such as making frozen cocktails).

Large baking sheets Every restaurant has a stack of 17 × 12-inch aluminum baking sheets. Called half-sheets (a full-sheet pan is twice as big), they can be used for everything from baking cookies to roasting vegetables and cut-up chicken.

Baking parchment To keep cookies and other pastries from sticking to baking sheets, parchment paper is an inexpensive solution. It also keeps the pans clean, so you can bake a couple of batches on the same sheet without cleaning them, a great time-saver. If you do a lot of baking, invest in silicone baking pads, available at kitchenware shops. These have the same nonstick qualities as parchment and can be reused about one thousand times before they finally wear out.

Pastry bag and tip Every home kitchen should have just one large, open star pastry tip with a ½-inch wide opening and a 12- to 14-inch pastry bag. I am not asking for a complete set of tips for cake decorating, just one pair of basic tools to add flair to your cooking. A tip-equipped pastry bag can pipe filling into deviled eggs, create swirls of whipped cream on desserts, and perform other decorative chores. Sometimes the difference between a dowdy-looking dessert and a showstopper is a simple topping of whipped cream rosettes.

Meat thermometer Do not try to second-guess the internal temperature of a roast. The only way to really check the doneness is with a meat thermometer. Old-fashioned meat thermometers can stay in the meat throughout roasting, but they create a rather large hole when removed. An instant-read thermometer should only be used to quickly check the temperature—it will melt if left in the oven. The new probe thermometers, with cords that run out of the oven into a digital readout, are very efficient, and you do not have to open the oven door to check the temperature. However, some older models of probe thermometers will burn out if used at temperatures over 392°F.

Carving set Roast meats and poultry make festive meals especially convivial. To simplify carving, use a good carving set. The knife should be long and sharp, with a thin, flexible blade and a pointed tip for cutting through tough joints. The meat fork should be sturdy with elongated tines to hold the meat steady. Even the best carving set will not be able to do its job if the blade is dull, so be sure to sharpen the knife well before putting it into use.

Electric juicer Now that I have an electric juicer on the kitchen counter, when a recipe calls for 1 cup of fresh lemon juice, it doesn't bother me in the least. These are inexpensive and can make child's play out of the tedious chore of squeezing citrus.

Large pitcher A 2-quart glass pitcher allows the bartender to mix up a big batch of the party's cocktails, and pour them as needed.

Punch bowl Sometimes a punch bowl is the best way to serve a beverage to a large group. The right punch recipe can set the mood for a party; offer your guests a cup of Plantation Punch, and they'll know it is Mardi Gras, all right. If you entertain often, a punch bowl is a worthwhile investment. I am not suggesting that everyone have a silver-plated bowl—inexpensive glass punch bowls are easy to find at kitchenware shops, or a large, attractive kitchen bowl can be pulled into service.

Warming plate A flat, electric warming plate will help keep hot dishes warm on a buffet.

Slow cookers Not just for all-day cooking, these crockery appliances also keep foods warm. For warm drinks like hot cider, use the 3½-quart model. The 1-quart model is perfect for hot dips.

Coffee servers Unless you regularly entertain large groups, you probably won't need a coffee urn, which makes upwards of 36 cups. It may be more convenient to use a thermal pump pot, the kind that coffee shops use to dispense hot beverages. Just make up a pot or two of coffee in your regular coffeemaker, pour into the pump pot, and you're all set.

Self-sealing plastic bags To store salads and other bulky foods, place them in zippered plastic bags. They'll take up much less room than a large bowl.

Serving platters and bowls Hard-core party cooks will want to have at least two large serving platters and two deep serving bowls. Colorful serving pieces are nice, but the truth is that all food looks good on white ceramic.

Part One

Kicking Off the
New Year

A New Year's Day Open House

A Super Bowl Bash

A Mardi Gras Celebration

A Happy Birthday Buffet

A New Year's Day Open House

New Year's Day is, of course, the beginning of the New Year, but it is also the close to the holiday party season. With the house still decorated and the tree still sparkling with lights, I like one more chance to

Serves 12

Baked Ham with Pineapple Chutney Glaze

Green Bean Salad with Toasted Pecan Vinaigrette

Yam and Yukon Gold Potato Salad

Fresh Rolls, Mustard, and Mayonnaise*

Jean's Flat Apple Pie

Five-Spice Hot Apple Cider

*Recipe not included

enjoy the special atmosphere. Plus, after all of the shopping, wrapping, and running around, the pressure is finally off. So, I throw open my doors for the day and invite friends over for a low-key meal. Because most people will have partied hard the night before, the atmosphere should be casual, and this menu has a down-home feel, as well.

The guests at my open house are usually people who have not recently been at any of my other holiday parties. Many of my friends travel during Christmastime, but they have made it back home by New Year's Day. This party lets me catch up with friends and family I may not have seen for a while.

At any open house, people will come and go over a few hours. Some will come for a full meal, others will just have a light bite. Smoked ham offers many possibilities. Offer fresh rolls, mayonnaise, and mustard on the table, and guests who just want a snack can make sandwiches. Those with larger appetites can load up a plate with sliced ham and the green bean and potato salads. A beautiful, glazed whole ham looks terrific on a buffet. The ham and salads can stay at room temperature for up to two hours, giving the host or hostess more time to spend with guests. If you think you are going to have the food out for longer than that, put out smaller amounts and replenish with fresh food every hour or so.

For appetizers, choose a couple of items from the Holiday Cocktail Party menu on page 267, or make your favorite dip. Keep the beverage selection simple and light on the alcohol. It's best to serve something nonalcoholic, like the five-spice hot apple cider, and let guests add their own rum if they wish.

Baked Ham with Pineapple Chutney Glaze

Makes 12 to 16 buffet servings
Make Ahead: The ham is best baked right before serving.

I'm always fussing with my baked ham recipe, looking to perfect the time-honored combination of rich smoky ham and sweet-tangy pineapple. I think I can stop experimenting now, because this version is just right. Always start with the best ham you can find, which should have a minimum of additional flavorings or glazes. I go out of my way to buy a shank-end half ham from a Polish butcher whose product is highly regarded, and it is worth the trip.

One 9-pound shank-end smoked ham, on the bone

Pineapple Chutney Glaze

1 tablespoon vegetable oil

⅓ cup minced onion

2 tablespoons grated fresh ginger (use the large holes on a box grater)

1 jalapeño, seeded and minced, or more to taste

2 garlic cloves, crushed through a press

1 cup pineapple preserves

1 tablespoon dry mustard

1. Position the rack in the center of the oven and preheat to 325°F. Line a large roasting pan with aluminum foil (this ensures easy cleanup) and lightly oil the foil.

2. Using a sharp knife, trim off all of the skin, leaving a 1- to 2-inch band around the shank. Trim off all of the fat, leaving a less than ¼-inch thick layer. Score the fat into a diamond pattern. Place the ham in the pan, with the cut, flat side down and the shank pointing straight up. Pour 3 cups of water into the pan.

3. Bake the ham, basting occasionally with the water in the pan, until a meat thermometer inserted in the thickest part of the ham without touching the bone reads 125°F, about 2½ hours.

4. Meanwhile, make the glaze. Heat the oil in a medium saucepan over medium heat. Add the onion, stirring often, until the onion is golden, about 5

minutes. Add the ginger, jalapeño, and garlic and cook until the garlic is fragrant, about 1 minute. Add the pineapple preserves and mustard. Heat to melt the preserves, stirring often. Set aside.

5. Remove the ham from the oven and generously brush the ham with the glaze. Return the ham to the oven and bake until the glaze is lightly browned, about 20 minutes. The internal temperature should be around 135°F—the temperature will rise 5 degrees or so as the ham rests outside of the oven.

6. Transfer the ham to a carving board or platter. Let stand for 15 to 45 minutes before carving (see page 16).

How to Carve a Ham

Recently, I decided to enter the twenty-first century and bake a spiral-sliced ham, a somewhat new addition to the supermarket shelves. After all, presliced ham would be perfect for a buffet. I wish I could recommend the results; the ham was excessively salty to my taste. It makes sense that presliced hams would be salty; they are injected with copious amounts of brine to compensate for the juices lost during processing. If you have a brand of presliced ham that you like (I cannot say that I have tried all brands, but the two I did try left me unimpressed), you can certainly use the pineapple chutney glaze on it. However, I am sticking to my whole, bone-in smoked ham, which means it needs to be sliced before serving.

Although a large ham may look daunting, it is easy to carve. The first rule is to let the meat stand for at least 15 minutes and up to 45 minutes before carving. It will cool only minimally—in fact, the temperature will first rise about 5 degrees from the residual heat. This allows the hot juices to soak back into the meat—if the ham is carved too soon, the juices will squirt out onto the platter, resulting in dry meat. (All of this also applies to any roast meat or large poultry.) If you want to serve cold ham, remember that it should not stand at room temperature for longer than 2 hours.

After the ham has rested, use a carving knife to cut a few slices from the less meaty side. Turn the ham to stand on its newly flattened side. Slice the ham as thinly as you like, cutting straight down to the bone, stopping a few inches from the end of the shank. Cut along the length of the bone to release the sliced ham. Cut the ham into serving pieces and arrange on a serving platter. When you need more slices, turn the ham over and slice the remaining ham in the same fashion.

Green Bean Salad with Toasted Pecan Vinaigrette

Makes 12 servings

Make Ahead: The green beans, vinaigrette, and pecans can be prepared 1 day ahead.

This refreshing salad goes perfectly with the ham. To make short work of trimming the green beans, use kitchen scissors.

2 pounds green beans, trimmed and cut into 2-inch lengths

¾ cup (3 ounces) pecan halves

2 tablespoons balsamic vinegar

2 tablespoons red wine vinegar

¾ cup vegetable oil

Salt and freshly ground black pepper, to taste

1. Bring a large pot of lightly salted water to a boil over high heat. Add the beans and cook until crisp-tender, about 3 minutes. Drain and rinse well under cold running water. Spread on paper towels and pat dry. Cool completely. (The green beans can be prepared up to 1 day ahead, wrapped in fresh, dry paper towels, placed in plastic bags, and refrigerated.)

2. Position a rack in the center of the oven and preheat to 350°F. Spread the pecans on a baking sheet. Bake, stirring occasionally, until toasted and fragrant, about 10 minutes. Cool completely. Coarsely chop ¼ cup of the pecans and set aside.

3. Combine the remaining ½ cup pecans and the balsamic and wine vinegars in a blender. With the machine running, gradually add the oil to make a smooth vinaigrette. Season with salt and pepper. (The vinaigrette and chopped pecans can be prepared up to 1 day ahead, covered, and refrigerated.)

4. Toss the green beans with the vinaigrette in a large bowl. Transfer to a serving platter or bowl and sprinkle with the chopped pecans. Serve chilled or at room temperature.

Yam and Yukon Gold Potato Salad

Makes 12 servings

Make Ahead: The salad can be prepared up to 1 day ahead, covered, and refrigerated.

On paper, yams (a.k.a. sweet potatoes) should make a great-tasting salad with a gorgeous golden color. However, my first attempts turned out mushy and cloyingly sweet. The answer to the problem turned out to be to use a combination of roasted yams (peeled before roasting so they retain their shape), boiled, waxy-fleshed potatoes (peeled after boiling, for the same reason), and a brightly acidic lemon vinaigrette to balance the sugary yams. Mint supplies a fresh note, but cilantro or parsley can be substituted. Use medium potatoes so they cook evenly and with relative speed.

2½ pounds medium orange-fleshed yams, such as Louisiana, jewel, or garnet, peeled and cut into 1½-inch chunks

1¼ cups plus 2 tablespoons olive oil (not extra virgin, which may be too rich), divided

3 pounds medium Yukon gold potatoes, scrubbed but unpeeled

¼ cup plus 2 tablespoons fresh lemon juice

1½ teaspoons dry mustard

1¼ teaspoons salt, plus more to taste

½ teaspoon freshly ground black pepper, plus more to taste

4 celery ribs, chopped

4 scallions, white and green parts, chopped

¼ cup chopped fresh mint, cilantro, or parsley

1. Position a rack in the center of the oven and preheat to 400°F. Toss the yam chunks with 2 tablespoons of the oil in a large bowl. Spread on a rimmed baking sheet. Bake, stirring occasionally, until the chunks are tender when pierced with the tip of a knife, about 45 minutes. Cool completely.

2. Meanwhile, place the potatoes in a large pot of lightly salted water and cover. Bring to a boil over high heat. Reduce the heat to medium and cook until the potatoes are tender enough to be pierced with the tip of a sharp knife, about 25 minutes. Drain and rinse under cold water until cool enough to handle. Peel the potatoes and cut into 1½-inch chunks.

3. Combine the lemon juice, mustard, salt, and pepper in a blender. With the machine running, gradually add the oil to make a thick vinaigrette.

4. Mix the yams, potatoes, celery, scallions, and mint in a large bowl. Toss with about three-fourths of the vinaigrette. Separately cover the salad and remaining vinaigrette and refrigerate both until the salad is chilled, at least 3 hours. (The salad and vinaigrette can be made up to 1 day ahead.)

5. Just before serving, toss the salad with the remaining vinaigrette and season with salt and pepper. Serve chilled.

Jean's Flat Apple Pie

Makes 12 servings

Make Ahead: The pie dough can be made up to 2 days ahead, wrapped in plastic wrap, and refrigerated. The pie is best served the day it is made, but it can be made 1 day ahead, loosely covered, and stored at cool room temperature.

This delicious hybrid, the specialty of my dear friend Jean Turpen, is one of those desserts that American bakers love—it is relatively easy, makes enough for a crowd, and is utterly irresistible. Baked in a jelly-roll pan, it's a cross between a cobbler, a pie, and a big cookie. The pie can made with just about any seasonal fruit—peaches, nectarines, and Italian purple plums are all excellent substitutes for the apples— adjusting the amount of sugar as needed. A layer of crushed cornflakes on the bottom crust soaks up and thickens the fruit juices so the consistency is always perfect.

Dough

3 cups all-purpose flour

¾ teaspoon salt

¾ cup chilled vegetable shortening, cut into ½-inch cubes (see Note)

8 tablespoons (1 stick) unsalted butter, cut into ½-inch cubes

1 large egg yolk (save the white for brushing the top dough)

⅔ cup milk, as needed

2½ cups cornflakes, crushed (place the cornflakes in a plastic bag and crush with a rolling pin)

3 pounds Golden Delicious apples, peeled, cored, and thinly sliced

½ cup granulated sugar

½ teaspoon ground cinnamon

2 tablespoons unsalted butter, thinly sliced

1 large egg white, beaten until foamy

Glaze

1 cup confectioners' sugar

½ teaspoon vanilla extract

1 tablespoon boiling water, as needed

1. To make the dough, whisk the flour and salt to combine in a large bowl. Using a pastry blender, cut in the vegetable shortening and butter until the mixture resembles coarse cornmeal. Mix the egg yolk and enough milk to make ¾ cup

liquid. Gradually stir the milk into the flour to make a dough that clumps to-gether (you may not need all of the milk). Gather up the dough and divide into two portions, one slightly larger than the other. Shape each portion of dough into a thick rectangle and wrap in plastic wrap. Refrigerate until chilled, about 1 hour. (The dough can be made up to 2 days ahead. Let stand at room temperature for about 10 minutes before rolling out.)

2. Position a rack in the center of the oven and preheat to 375°F.

3. On a lightly floured surface, roll out the larger dough portion into a thin 17 × 12-inch rectangle. Transfer to a 15 × 10 × 1-inch jelly-roll pan, letting the excess hang over the edges. If the dough cracks, just piece and press it back together. Distribute the cornflakes evenly over the dough. Arrange the apples in a layer over the cornflakes. Sprinkle with the sugar and cinnamon, then dot with the butter. Roll out the smaller dough portion into a thin 16 × 11-inch rectangle and place over the apples. Again, don't worry if the dough cracks; just patch it up. Pinch the edges of the dough together to seal. Cut a few slits in the top of the dough and brush lightly with some of the beaten egg white.

4. Bake until the crust is golden brown and the apples feel tender when pierced through the slits in the crust with the tip of a small knife, about 45 minutes. Cool completely on a wire rack.

5. When the pie is cool, make the glaze. Sift the confectioners' sugar into a small bowl. Add the vanilla. Stir in enough boiling water to make a glaze about the consistency of heavy cream. Drizzle the glaze over the pie, then brush it into a thin layer with a pastry brush. Let the glaze set, about 30 minutes. To serve, cut the pie into large squares.

Note: If you are concerned about the trans-fatty acids in vegetable shortening, substitute an additional 12 tablespoons of unsalted butter, cut into ½-inch cubes, for the shortening. The baked crust will not be as flaky or tender, but it will be delicious.

Five-Spice Hot Apple Cider

Makes 2 quarts, about 16 servings
Make Ahead: The cider is best prepared just before serving.

Hot apple cider fills the entire house with a welcoming, spicy aroma. The spices here are a bit more exotic than the usual blend. You can find star anise and Sichuan peppercorns at Asian grocers and many supermarkets. Serve the rum on the side so guests can add as much as they wish, if any at all.

8 quarter-sized slices fresh ginger

8 whole star anise pods

Four 3-inch long cinnamon sticks

2 teaspoons Sichuan peppercorns, optional

1 teaspoon whole cloves

½ teaspoon fennel seeds

2 quarts fresh apple cider

Dark rum, for serving

1. Rinse a 12-inch square piece of cheesecloth under cold water and squeeze it dry. (This removes any sizing from the cloth.) Wrap the ginger, star anise, cinnamon sticks, optional peppercorns, cloves, and fennel in the cheesecloth and tie it with kitchen string.

2. Combine the cider and wrapped spices in a large nonaluminum pot. Heat over medium-low heat, stirring occasionally, just until hot but not boiling, about 30 minutes. Transfer to a slow cooker or warming plate set on Low and serve hot.

A New Year's Day Open House Shopping List

Serves 12

Dairy

Fresh apple cider (2 quarts)

Unsalted butter (1¼ sticks)

Large eggs (1)

Milk (⅔ cup, as needed)

Dried Herbs and Spices

Cinnamon sticks (four 3-inch long)

Ground cinnamon (½ teaspoon)

Whole cloves (1 teaspoon)

Fennel seeds (½ teaspoon)

Dry mustard (1½ tablespoons)

Sichuan peppercorns (2 teaspoons)

Star anise (8 whole pods)

Groceries

Cornflakes (about 2½ cups)

Pecan halves (3 ounces)

Pineapple preserves (one 12-ounce jar)

Vegetable shortening (¾ cup)

Liquor

Dark rum (1 quart)

Meat

Smoked ham, shank end, with bone (one
  9-pound)

Pantry Staples

Olive oil (about 1¼ cups)

Vegetable oil (about 1¼ cups)

Balsamic vinegar (2 tablespoons)

Red wine vinegar (2 tablespoons)

All-purpose flour (3 cups)

Confectioners' sugar (1 cup)

Granulated sugar (½ cup)

Vanilla extract (½ teaspoon)

Produce

Golden Delicious apples (3 pounds)

Celery (1 head)

Garlic (1 head)

Ginger (8 ounces)

Green beans (2 pounds)

Jalapeño (1)

Lemons (3 medium, for 6 tablespoons fresh
  lemon juice)

Mint (1 bunch, for ¼ cup chopped)

Yukon Gold potatoes (3 pounds medium)

Scallions (1 bunch)

Orange-fleshed yams, also called sweet
  potatoes (2½ pounds medium)

Yellow onions (1 small)

A New Year's Day Open House Preparation Timetable

2 days before serving

    Make dough for flat apple pie; refrigerate

1 day before serving

    Blanch green beans; refrigerate

    Make vinaigrette for green beans; refrigerate

    Make potato salad; refrigerate

8 hours before serving

    Make filling and finish flat apple pie

    Cool and glaze flat apple pie

4 hours before serving

    Bake ham; make glaze; glaze ham; let stand 15 to 45 minutes before carving

About 30 minutes before serving

    Heat apple cider; keep warm

Just before serving

    Carve ham

    Toss green beans with vinaigrette, sprinkle with pecans

    Add remaining dressing to potato salad; adjust seasoning

A Super Bowl Bash

A Super Bowl Bash By late January, it is likely weeks since you last went to a good party. The weather is boring (where I live, make that boring and cold). You need a little excitement in your social life.

Even if you aren't a football fan, a Super Bowl party is always a lot of fun. If you don't catch the annual batch of outra-

Serves 10 to 12

Layered Guacamole Dip with Shrimp and Salsa
Roasted Buffalo Wings with Blue Cheese Dip
Blue-Ribbon Chunky Chili
Omigod! Brownies

geous commercials or the halftime entertainment, you won't be able to take part in the water cooler discussions the next day at work.

There are a few ground rules for Super Bowl parties. First, guests need to be able to watch television and eat at the same time. Therefore, finger food, or at least easy-to-eat food, is the order of the day. (I've served this menu at other TV-watching parties, like the Oscars, as well.) If there is such a thing as masculine food, now is the time to serve it. I've painted the flavors in this menu with very broad strokes, as it were, with plenty of heat and spice.

At any Super Bowl, no matter what teams are playing or how many people there know a touchdown from a home run, food is an enormous part of the fun. My friends Joel and Cheryl always serve a huge pot of chili, which is easy to eat out of coffee mugs with spoons. My cousin Elizabeth and her husband, Mike, change the bill of fare every year, but you can be sure that she will make a mountain of seafood dip. I've taken their leads, and added roasted chicken wings, Buffalo-style, and outrageous thick-and-fudgy brownies for the fourth quarter. Pour cold beer, and plenty of it, all the better to wash down those chiles.

Layered Guacamole Dip with Shrimp and Salsa

Makes 10 to 12 servings

Make Ahead: The guacamole can be prepared 1 day ahead. Layer the components to make the dip up to 4 hours ahead, cover, and refrigerate.

Here's an updated version of the layered taco dip, the kind that usually uses canned refried beans and packaged taco seasonings. This rendition, with shrimp, is lighter and brighter in flavor. To save time, use cooked shrimp from the supermarket seafood counter. Ripe, dark, and pebbly-skinned Hass avocados make the best guacamole, as the larger, bright green, smooth-skinned varieties don't have nearly as much flavor. Sour cream in the guacamole discourages discoloring, so you can make it ahead without worry. If you're lucky enough to have leftover guacamole, use it as a sandwich spread.

Guacamole

3 ripe Hass avocados (see Note), pitted and peeled

½ cup sour cream

2 tablespoons fresh lime juice

¼ cup minced onion

2 garlic cloves, crushed through a press

Salt, to taste

1 pound cooked, peeled, and deveined shrimp, coarsely chopped

2 tablespoons olive oil, preferably extra virgin

2 teaspoons fresh lime juice

1 cup store-bought thick-and-chunky salsa

½ cup sour cream

2 tablespoons chopped fresh cilantro

Tortilla chips, for serving

1. To make the guacamole, mash the avocados, sour cream, and lime juice in a medium bowl with a slotted spoon or large serving fork until the mixture is chunky. Fold in the onion and garlic, and season generously with the salt. Cover tightly with plastic wrap and refrigerate until chilled, at least 2 hours. (The guacamole can be made up to 1 day ahead.)

2. Toss the shrimp with the oil and lime juice. Spread the shrimp in a thick layer about 9 inches in diameter on a rimmed serving platter. Spread the guacamole

on the shrimp, leaving a border exposed. Spread the salsa over the guacamole, leaving a border. Finally, spread the sour cream on the salsa, again leaving a border around the edges. Sprinkle the cilantro over the dip. (The dip can be prepared up to 4 hours ahead, covered tightly with plastic wrap, and refrigerated.) Serve chilled, with tortilla chips.

Note: It is not easy to find ripe avocados at the market; more often than not, they need a couple of days of ripening at home. Remember to buy the avocados a few days before making the guacamole. To hasten their ripening, place the hard avocados in a brown paper bag with a ripe banana or an apple. As the fruit continues to ripen, it will give off a gas that will in turn ripen the avocados. This trick cuts the ripening time in half.

Roasted Buffalo Wings with Blue Cheese—Celery Dip

Makes 10 to 12 servings

Make Ahead: The dip can be prepared up to 3 days ahead and refrigerated. The wings can be roasted and refrigerated up to 6 hours ahead, and reheated just before serving.

According to a recent poll, Buffalo wings are giving dips a run for their money as favorite Super Bowl fare. Classically, they are deep-fried, but when you need a mountain of wings for a crowd, roasting is much easier, and there is hardly any difference in flavor. The real fun is in choosing the hot sauce for coating the wings. Shop for an interesting new brand, or mix different sauces to create a blend with just the right kick. Or divide the wings and melted butter and make two or even three different flavors.

1 cup mayonnaise

½ cup sour cream

⅔ cup (3 ounces) crumbled blue cheese, such as Danish blue or Roquefort

1 medium celery rib with leaves, minced

1 scallion, white and green part, minced

¾ teaspoon freshly ground black pepper, divided

5¾ pounds fresh chicken wings, cut between the joints to make three pieces, wing tips reserved for another use (such as chicken stock), or 5 pounds thawed frozen chicken drummettes

1½ teaspoons salt

4 tablespoons (½ stick) unsalted butter

3 tablespoons hot pepper sauce

1. To make the dip, mix the mayonnaise, sour cream, and blue cheese in a medium bowl. Mix with a rubber spatula, mashing about half of the blue cheese until smooth. Stir in the celery, scallion, and ¼ teaspoon pepper. Cover and refrigerate until chilled, at least 1 hour or up to 3 days.

2. Position racks in the top third and center of the oven and preheat to 400°F.

3. Spread the wings in an even layer on two large rimmed baking sheets. Season with the salt and ½ teaspoon pepper. Bake, scraping the wings from the baking sheet with a metal spatula and turning them every 20 minutes, and switching the positions of the sheets from top to bottom halfway through bak-

ing, until the wings are crisp and golden brown, 50 minutes to 1 hour. (The wings can be prepared up to 6 hours ahead, cooled, covered, and refrigerated. Reheat on a single baking sheet or roasting pan in a preheated 425°F oven, turning occasionally, until heated through, about 10 minutes.) Transfer the wings to a large bowl.

4. Melt the butter in a small saucepan. Remove from the heat and whisk in the hot sauce. Pour over the wings and toss well to coat. Transfer the wings to a large platter and serve hot with the blue cheese dip and a bowl to collect the bones.

Chicken Wings

Frozen chicken drummettes (chicken wings cut between the joints into portions that look like mini-drumsticks) are available at many supermarkets and wholesale price clubs. Economically priced, they seem like a bargain over fresh wings and don't require any extra work. However, the cooking instructions call for baking the unthawed wings, and that almost guarantees a soggy result. It is much better to thaw the drummettes on large baking sheets in the refrigerator overnight. Before using, pat completely dry with paper towels.

Blue-Ribbon Chili

Makes 10 to 12 servings
Make Ahead: The chili can be made up to 2 days ahead, cooled, covered, and refrigerated, or frozen for up to 3 months.

Cooks can get into very heated arguments over how to make chili—tomatoes or no tomatoes; beans or not; stew meat over ground meat—and so on. The bottom line is that there are no set rules, so I make my bowl of red with everything. There are no shortcuts to great chili, but at least you have a heap of it when you're finished. Because this chili is so flavorful, I resist the temptation to offer the traditional toppings of sour cream, shredded Cheddar cheese, pickled jalapeño rings, chopped onions, and the like, but you can do so if you wish. It's your party.

6 bacon slices, coarsely chopped

5 pounds boneless beef chuck, cut into 1-inch cubes

2 tablespoons vegetable oil

3 medium onions, chopped

1 green bell pepper, seeds and ribs discarded, chopped

1 red bell pepper, seeds and ribs discarded, chopped

2 jalapeños, seeds and ribs discarded, minced

6 garlic cloves, minced

⅓ cup plus 1 tablespoon chili powder, preferably Gebhardt's, or use pure ground mild chile, such as ancho

2 tablespoons smoky Spanish paprika, such as pimentón de la Vera, or sweet Hungarian paprika

1 tablespoon ground cumin

1 tablespoon dried oregano

1 tablespoon salt, plus more to taste

½ teaspoon freshly ground black pepper

One 14½-ounce can diced tomatoes with juice

One 14½-ounce can beef broth, preferably reduced-sodium

One 12-ounce bottle lager beer

One 28-ounce can pinto beans, drained and rinsed

One 28-ounce can hominy, drained and rinsed

1. Cook the bacon in a large Dutch oven or flameproof casserole over medium heat, stirring occasionally, until crisp, about 8 minutes. Using a slotted spoon, transfer the bacon to paper towels to drain. *(continued)*

2. Increase the heat to medium-high. In batches without crowding, cook the beef cubes, turning occasionally, until browned on all sides, about 5 minutes. Using a slotted spoon, transfer the beef to a platter. The beef should give off enough fat and juices to brown, but if needed, add some of the vegetable oil to the pot.

3. Add the oil to the pot and heat. Stir in the onions, green and red bell peppers, jalapeños, and garlic, and return the heat to medium. Cover and cook, stirring occasionally, until the vegetables soften, about 10 minutes.

4. Return the meat and any juices on the platter to the pot. Sprinkle with the chili powder, paprika, cumin, oregano, salt, and pepper, and mix well. Stir in the tomatoes with their juices, the beef broth, and beer. Bring to a boil over high heat. Reduce the heat to medium-low. Cover and simmer until the beef is tender, about 1¾ hours. During the last 20 minutes, stir in the reserved bacon, beans, and hominy.

5. Remove the chili from the heat and let stand 10 minutes. Skim off any fat that rises to surface. If you like thick chili, return the chili to medium heat and bring to a simmer. Mash some of the beans and hominy into the sauce with a slotted spoon to thicken the juices. Adjust the seasoning with additional salt. (The chili can be made up to 2 days ahead, cooled, covered, and refrigerated, or frozen for up to 3 months.) Serve hot.

Chili Powder, Ground Chiles, and Smoked Paprika

When making chili, the quality of the spices is very important, because you are using a fairly large quantity. Chili powder is a blend of mild ground chiles mixed with other spices such as cumin, oregano, and garlic powder. I prefer Gebhardt's, a reliable Texan brand that I grew up with, but you can experiment with others. Watch out for the "hot" varieties, as they can make your chili too incendiary for everyone in the party to enjoy. You may also use pure ground chile, which is processed into a powder without any additional seasonings, but use a mild chile, such as ancho, New Mexican Hatch, or California. You can always add more heat with a touch of ground chipotle or even cayenne. Spanish smoked paprika has recently hit the market, and it is a great way to add a smoky flavor to food. You'll find it at high-quality kitchen shops.

Omigod! Brownies

Makes 16 brownies

Make Ahead: The brownies can be made up to 2 days ahead, individually wrapped in plastic wrap, and stored at room temperature.

If you like your brownies thick, fudgy, chewy, moist, nutty, and as chocolatey as humanly possible, these are the ones for you. For extra-fudgy brownies, wrap them tightly in plastic wrap and refrigerate overnight. I rarely serve these without getting some kind of amazed exclamation (usually a long, drawn-out "Oh . . . my . . . God!") from the person on the receiving end of the brownie.

1 cup (2 sticks) unsalted butter, cut up, plus softened butter for the pan

11 ounces semisweet chocolate, coarsely chopped

1 cup packed light brown sugar

¾ cup granulated sugar

¼ cup light corn syrup or honey

4 large eggs, at room temperature

2 teaspoons vanilla extract

2 cups all-purpose flour, plus more for the pan

2 cups (8 ounces) coarsely chopped pecans, divided

½ teaspoon baking soda

½ teaspoon salt

1 cup (6 ounces) semisweet chocolate chips

1. Position a rack in the center of the oven and preheat the oven to 350°F. Lightly butter a 13 × 9-inch baking pan. Fold an 18-inch-long piece of aluminum foil in half. Use the foil to line the bottom and short sides of the baking pan. Fold the foil hanging over the two ends to make "handles." Dust the exposed areas of the pan with flour and tap out the excess.

2. Melt the butter in a large saucepan over medium heat. Remove from the heat and stir in the chopped chocolate. Let stand until the chocolate softens, about 3 minutes, then whisk until smooth. Whisk in the brown and granulated sugars and corn syrup. One at a time, whisk in the eggs, then the vanilla.

3. Process the flour, ½ cup of the pecans, the baking soda, and salt in a food processor until the pecans are ground into a powder. Add to the chocolate mixture in the pan and mix until combined. Stir in the remaining 1½ cups pecans and the chocolate chips. Spread evenly in the pan.

4. Bake just until a toothpick inserted in the center of the brownie comes out with a moist crumb, about 45 minutes. Do not overbake. Cool *completely* on a wire cake rack.

5. Run a knife between the brownie and the pan to release the brownie. Lift up on the foil handles to remove the brownie in one piece. Peel off and discard the foil. Cut the brownie into 16 pieces. (The brownies can be made up to 2 days ahead, individually wrapped in plastic wrap, and stored at room temperature. Or overwrap the plastic-wrapped brownies in aluminum foil, and freeze for up to 1 month.)

A Super Bowl Bash Shopping List

Serves 10 to 12

Dairy

Blue cheese (3 ounces)

Unsalted butter (2½ sticks)

Large eggs (4)

Sour cream (1 pint)

Dried Herbs and Spices

Chili powder (⅓ cup plus 1 tablespoon)

Ground cumin (1 tablespoon)

Dried oregano (1 tablespoon)

Smoky Spanish paprika (2 tablespoons)

Fish

1 pound cooked, peeled, and deveined shrimp

Groceries

Beef broth, preferably reduced-sodium (one
14½-ounce can)

Semisweet chocolate (17 ounces)

Hominy (one 28-ounce can)

Mayonnaise (1 cup)

Pecans (8 ounces)

Pinto beans (one 28-ounce can)

Thick-and-chunky salsa (1 cup)

Tomatoes, diced with juice (one 14½-ounce can)

Tortilla chips (2 bags)

Liquor

Lager beer (one 12-ounce bottle)

Meat

Sliced bacon (6 slices)

Boneless beef chuck (5 pounds)

Fresh chicken wings (5¾ pounds) or frozen
chicken drummettes (5 pounds)

Pantry Staples

Baking soda (½ teaspoon)

Light brown sugar (1 cup)

Granulated sugar (¾ cup)

Hot pepper sauce (3 tablespoons)

All-purpose flour (2 cups)

Light corn syrup or honey (¼ cup)

Extra virgin olive oil (2 tablespoons)

Vegetable oil (2 tablespoons)

Vanilla extract (2 teaspoons)

Produce

Hass avocados (3 ripe)

Celery (1 rib)

Cilantro (1 bunch)

Garlic (1 head)

Green bell pepper (1)

Jalapeños (2)

Limes (2 each, for about ¼ cup fresh lime juice)

Red bell pepper (1)

Scallion (1)

Yellow onions (1 small, 3 medium)

A Super Bowl Bash Preparation Timetable

3 days before serving

Make blue cheese dip; refrigerate

2 days before serving

Bake brownies; wrap and refrigerate

Make chili; refrigerate

1 day before serving

Make guacamole

6 hours before serving

Roast chicken wings; refrigerate

4 hours before serving

Finish dip; refrigerate

Just before serving

Reheat chicken wings

Reheat chili

A Mardi Gras Celebration

I once wrote a cookbook in collaboration with a company based in New Orleans, and I got to know that city very well. Of the many observations I made about the Crescent City, the most impressive was the eating and drinking habits of my new friends.

Serves 10 to 12

Warm Red Bean and Andouille Dip

Chicken and Shrimp Étouffée

Shallot Rice

Cajun Ratatouille

Sweet Potato King Cake

Plantation Punch

I (barely) remember one of my lunch meetings with my clients. We went to their favorite place for lunch. Upon sitting down, the waitress brought their standing order of pre-lunch Bloody Marys. I declined wine with lunch—my hosts looked at me like I was out of my mind, and ordered a very good bottle to tempt me, and I gave in. Under the excuse that it was a cool winter afternoon (about 70°F, but that's cool in New Orleans), we ordered a round of post-dessert cafés brûlot, a flaming concoction of coffee, brandy, and spices. We didn't work much when we got back to the office, because most of the discussion concerned where we were going to go to dinner that night!

In addition to its unrestrained adoration of the local cuisine, New Orleans is famous for another indulgence—Mardi Gras. While it is certainly fun to experience Mardi Gras in New Orleans, there's no reason why you can't let the good times roll wherever you live.

Historically, Fat Tuesday serves as a way to let off steam before the deprivation of Lent. I use it as another way to lift mid-winter doldrums and as an excuse to cook up some of my favorite Cajun/Creole dishes. It's kind of difficult to complain about the cold weather listening to Dixieland jazz with a mouthful of étouffée and wearing a bead necklace. If you wish, you can go whole hog and require costumes of your guests, but that's a challenge that you may not care to present. It's a lot easier to find the perfect costume in October than January or February.

Many Cajun and Creole recipes use the "holy quintet" of onion, scallions, celery, green peppers, and garlic as basic seasoning. If you are cooking the entire menu on the same day, you may find it helpful to "mise en place" these ingredients. In other words, chop the total amount of each vegetable required for the entire menu (chop all three onions, for example), then use them as needed.

Warm Red Bean and Andouille Dip

Makes 10 to 12 servings

Make Ahead: The dip can be made up to 1 day ahead. Reheat gently over low heat.

This hearty spread can be served with a variety of dippers, from fresh baguette slices to sturdy tortilla chips, but Baguette Crisps (recipe follows) are perfect. Serve the dip warm in a chafing dish (replace the fuel unit with a votive candle, which will keep the dip warm without excess heat) or a 1-quart electric slow cooker.

1 tablespoon olive oil, preferably extra virgin

½ pound andouille or hot links sausage, cut into ¼-inch
    dice

1 small onion, chopped

2 scallions, white and green parts, chopped

½ cup finely chopped red bell pepper

2 garlic cloves, minced

1 tablespoon Cajun Seasoning (recipe follows)

Two 15- to 19-ounce cans red beans, drained, *liquid
    reserved*

Hot red pepper sauce, to taste

Baguette Crisps (opposite page) or baguette slices

1. Heat the oil in a large nonstick skillet over medium-high heat. Add the andouille and cook, turning often, until browned, about 5 minutes. Add the onion, scallions, red bell pepper, and garlic, and reduce the heat to medium. Cover and cook until the vegetables are tender, about 5 minutes.

2. Stir in the Cajun seasoning. Add the beans and cook, stirring often, until heated through, about 3 minutes. Using a slotted spoon or a potato masher, mash the beans in the skillet, adding enough of the reserved bean liquid as needed. Season with the hot pepper sauce. (The dip can be made up to 1 day ahead, cooled, covered, and refrigerated. Reheat in the skillet over low heat, adding water as needed to soften the dip to dipping consistency.)

3. Transfer the dip to a chafing dish or small electric slow cooker. Serve warm, with the crisps.

Cajun Seasoning Mix 2 tablespoons sweet Hungarian paprika, 1 tablespoon each dried basil and dried thyme, 1 teaspoon each garlic powder and onion powder, ¼ teaspoon freshly ground black pepper, and ¼ teaspoon ground hot red (cayenne) pepper. Store in an airtight container in a cool dark place. Makes about ⅓ cup.

Baguette Crisps

These crunchy toasted bread slices are great for dipping, serving with cheese, or even snacking.

For garlic-flavored crisps, heat ⅓ cup extra virgin olive oil and 2 large garlic cloves, crushed under a knife, in a small saucepan until small bubbles appear around the edges. Remove from the heat and let stand for 10 minutes. Strain the oil, discarding the garlic. Slice a long, thin baguette into ¼-inch thick slices and place the slices in a large bowl. Drizzle the oil over the slices, tossing them well. Spread the slices on a baking sheet. Bake in a preheated 400°F oven until crisp and golden, 12 to 15 minutes. Cool.

For plain crisps, delete the garlic.

To store, place the crisps in a brown paper bag (storing in plastic can make the crisps soggy), close the bag, and store at room temperature for up to 8 hours.

Chicken and Shrimp Étouffée

Makes 10 to 12 servings

Make Ahead: The étouffée can be partially prepared up to 4 hours ahead.

"Smothered" chicken and shrimp is a perfect illustration of how New Orleans cooks coax flavor from humble ingredients. Note that there aren't a lot of herbs or spices here, just a savvy combination of vegetables and a quick roux. The traditional roux cooks butter and flour together until the mixture turns dark brown, but I prefer toasting the flour separately, which saves time and increases the cook's control over the process.

2 pounds large (21 to 25 count) shrimp (see Note)

One 14½-ounce can reduced-sodium chicken broth

1½ cups dry white wine

½ cup all-purpose flour

4 pounds boneless skinless chicken breasts, cut into
   1½-inch pieces

¾ teaspoon salt, plus more to taste

½ teaspoon freshly ground black pepper, plus more to
   taste

2 tablespoons vegetable oil, as needed

8 tablespoons (1 stick) unsalted butter

1 large onion, finely chopped

3 scallions, white and green parts, chopped

6 medium celery ribs, chopped into ¼-inch dice

1 large red bell pepper, seeded and chopped into ¼-inch
   dice

3 garlic cloves, minced

Hot red pepper sauce, to taste

3 tablespoons chopped fresh parsley, for garnish

Shallot Rice (page 44)

1. Peel and devein the shrimp, reserving the shells. Cover and refrigerate the shrimp. Combine the shrimp shells, broth, and wine in a medium saucepan. Add enough cold water to cover the shells by 1 inch. Bring to a boil over high heat. Reduce the heat to low and partially cover. Simmer for 15 minutes. Strain and reserve the stock. You should have 5 cups; add water if needed.

2. Heat an empty medium skillet over medium heat. Add the flour and cook, stirring occasionally, until the flour is toasted to a medium brown, about 5 min-

utes. Transfer the flour to a plate (if allowed to stand in the skillet, it will continue cooking and could burn).

3. Season the chicken with the salt and pepper. Heat the oil in a large Dutch oven or flameproof casserole over medium-high heat. In batches, without crowding and adding more oil as needed, add the chicken to the pot and cook, turning occasionally, until lightly browned, about 5 minutes. Using a slotted spoon, transfer the chicken to a platter. (The chicken can be prepared up to this point 4 hours ahead. Cool, cover, and refrigerate.)

4. Reduce the heat to medium. Add the butter to the pot and melt it. Add the onion, scallions, celery, red bell pepper, and garlic, and cover. Cook, stirring occasionally, until the vegetables are tender, about 10 minutes. Add the browned flour and stir well. Stir in the stock and bring to a boil. Reduce the heat to medium-low and simmer until the sauce is slightly thickened, about 20 minutes. (The dish can be made up to this point up to 4 hours ahead, cooled, covered, and refrigerated. Before continuing, bring the sauce to a simmer over low heat.)

5. Stir the chicken, and any juices on the platter into the sauce and return the sauce to a simmer. Cook, stirring often, for 3 minutes. Stir in the shrimp and cook just until the shrimp are pink and opaque and the chicken is cooked through, about 5 minutes. Season the sauce with salt and the red pepper sauce.

6. Transfer to a deep serving platter and sprinkle with the parsley. Serve hot, spooned over the rice.

Note: I rarely buy shelled and deveined shrimp because I like having the shells to make a quick shellfish sauce. However, shelled shrimp are convenient and a time saver (I do use them in the Layered Guacamole Dip with Shrimp and Salsa on page 27). If you wish, purchase shelled shrimp and skip the step of simmering the shells in the broth.

Shallot Rice

Makes 10 to 12 servings

Make Ahead: The rice is best prepared just before serving, but can be kept hot, covered, for 20 minutes.

Many dishes call for a bed of tasty, fluffy rice; with étouffée, it's de rigueur. For the most perfect rice with separate grains, use converted rice. It's been precooked, so much of the starch that causes sticky rice has been eliminated. Shallots, wine, and broth all contribute flavor to make this a side dish out of the ordinary. You could make this rice ahead of time and reheat it in the oven, but it is so easy that reheating simply complicates matters.

2 tablespoons unsalted butter

1 cup chopped shallots

3 cups long-grain rice, preferably converted

Two 14½-ounce cans reduced-sodium chicken broth

1 cup dry white wine

2 teaspoons salt

1. Melt the butter in a large saucepan over medium-high heat. Add the shallots and cook, stirring often, until softened, about 3 minutes. Add the rice and stir well.

2. Add the broth, 1½ cups water, the wine, and salt, and bring to a boil over high heat. Cover tightly and reduce the heat to low. Cook until the rice is tender and has absorbed all of the liquid, about 20 minutes. Remove from the heat and let stand for 5 minutes. (Covered tightly, the rice will stay hot for about 20 minutes.)

3. Fluff the rice with a fork. Transfer to a serving dish and serve hot.

Cajun Ratatouille

Makes 10 to 12 servings

Make Ahead: The ratatouille can be made 2 days ahead, cooled, covered, and refrigerated.

Eggplants, peppers, zucchini, tomatoes, and onions are all favorite vegetables in Louisiana kitchens. Because so much of the bayou was settled by French-speaking folk, it's not surprising that these vegetables are also components of many French dishes, including ratatouille. With a bit of bayou-style seasoning, this vegetable stew goes Cajun.

2 medium eggplants, cut into 1-inch chunks

1 teaspoon salt, plus more for seasoning

6 tablespoons extra virgin olive oil, divided

1 large onion, chopped

1 medium celery rib with leaves, chopped

2 scallions, white and green parts, chopped

1 small green bell pepper, seeded and chopped

2 garlic cloves, chopped

1 tablespoon Cajun Seasoning (page 41) or use store-bought, salt-free Cajun-Creole seasoning

One 28-ounce can diced tomatoes in juice (juices reserved)

2 medium zucchini, cut in half lengthwise, then crosswise into ½-inch lengths

1. Toss the eggplant and salt in a colander and let drain in a sink for 30 to 60 minutes. Rinse well with cold water. Pat the eggplant dry with paper towels.

2. Meanwhile, heat 2 tablespoons oil in a large saucepan over medium heat. Add the onion, celery, scallions, bell pepper, and garlic and cover. Cook, stirring occasionally, until the vegetables are tender, about 12 minutes. Sprinkle with the Cajun Seasoning and stir well. Stir in the tomatoes with their juices and bring to a boil. Reduce the heat to low. Simmer, uncovered, stirring often, until the sauce has reduced slightly, about 25 minutes. Keep the sauce warm.

3. Position racks in the center and top third of the oven and preheat to 425°F. Lightly oil two large baking sheets.

4. Toss the eggplant with 2 tablespoons oil on one oiled baking sheet and spread in a single layer. Toss the zucchini with 2 tablespoons oil on the other

large baking sheet and spread in a single layer. Bake the eggplant and zucchini, stirring occasionally, until lightly browned and tender, about 45 minutes. Add to the tomato sauce and bring to a simmer. Cook for 5 minutes. (The ratatouille can be made 2 days ahead, cooled, covered, and refrigerated. Reheat gently in a large skillet over low heat with a little water.)

5. Season the ratatouille with salt. Transfer to a serving dish and serve hot.

Sweet Potato King Cake

Makes 12 servings
Make Ahead: The cake can be made 1 day ahead.

During Mardi Gras in New Orleans, every bakery sells King Cake, a sweet yeast ring decorated with gold, green, and purple sugars, the official colors of the holiday. I tested a number of traditional King Cakes for this book, but they required bread-making skill and weren't any improvement over the ones you can mail-order from a bakery. So I've taken one of my favorite cake recipes from the Southern kitchen, and gussied it up Mardi Gras-style. Sweet potatoes make this a moist cake, one that may remind you of carrot cake. Use the large holes on a box grater to shred the yams. If you don't want to use the bourbon, use orange juice.

Cake

Butter and dried bread crumbs, for the pan

2½ cups all-purpose flour

1 tablespoon baking powder

1 teaspoon ground cinnamon

1 teaspoon freshly grated nutmeg

½ teaspoon salt

1½ cups vegetable oil

2 cups granulated sugar

4 large eggs, at room temperature

Grated zest of 1 orange

¼ cup bourbon or fresh orange juice

1½ cups peeled and shredded orange-fleshed yams, such as Louisiana, garnet, or jewel (about 1 large yam)

One 20-ounce can crushed pineapple in juice, well drained

1 cup coarsely chopped pecans

1 cup golden or dark raisins

Icing

1 cup confectioners' sugar

2 tablespoons bourbon or fresh orange juice

Water, as needed

Yellow, green, and purple decorating sugars (see Note)

1. To make the cake, position a rack in the center of the oven and preheat to 350°F (325°F if using a dark pan). Lightly butter a 10-inch fluted tube pan. Coat the inside of the pan with bread crumbs and tap out the excess crumbs, even if the pan it is nonstick.

(continued)

2. Sift the flour, baking powder, cinnamon, nutmeg, and salt. Using an electric mixer on high speed, beat the oil and sugar until combined. One at a time, beat in the eggs, then the orange zest and bourbon. On low speed, add the flour in three additions. Stir in the sweet potatoes, drained pineapple, pecans, and raisins. Spread evenly in the pan.

3. Bake until the cracks in the surface of the cake seem dry and the cake is beginning to shrink from the sides of the pan, about 1 hour (about 1¼ hours if using a dark pan at 325°F). Transfer to a wire cake rack and cool for 10 minutes. Invert and unmold the cake onto the rack and cool completely.

4. To make the icing, whisk the confectioners' sugar, bourbon, and enough water as needed, 1 teaspoon at a time, to make an icing with the consistency of thick heavy cream.

5. Place the cake, flat side down, on the rack, over a rimmed baking sheet. Slowly pour the icing over the top of the cake to coat as evenly as possible, letting the icing run down the sides of the cake. Sprinkle each colored sugar over the cake to make alternating toppings of yellow, green, and purple. Let the icing stand until firm, about 1 hour. (The cake can be made 1 day ahead, wrapped in plastic wrap, and stored at room temperature.)

Note: Search out the yellow, green, and purple decorating sugars at kitchenware or bakery suppliers well before you bake the cake. They are very popular during Mardi Gras and can be hard to find, even outside of Louisiana. In a pinch, make your own. Place a few tablespoons of coarse (also known as sanding sugar) or granulated sugar in a small plastic bag. Add a couple of drops of food coloring, preferably food-coloring paste (to make purple, mix 2 drops red and 1 blue), close the bag, and knead the sugar through the bag until it is evenly colored. Spread each sugar onto wax paper, and let stand overnight to dry completely.

Plantation Punch

Makes 2 quarts, 12 to 16 servings

Make Ahead: The punch can be made up to 1 day ahead, covered, and refrigerated.

This fruity punch has a long Southern tradition of being a superior way to welcome guests with a tasty, if potent, libation. It is best made with freshly squeezed juices, so use an inexpensive reamer-style electric juicer for the limes and lemons, but fresh orange juice from the dairy section is fine.

3 cups fresh orange juice

3 cups canned unsweetened pineapple juice

1½ cups fresh lemon juice

1½ cups fresh lime juice

¾ cup superfine sugar

¾ cup grenadine

1 ripe pineapple, pared, cored, and cut into 1-inch cubes

1½ cups golden or dark rum

1. The night before serving, mix the orange, pineapple, lemon, and lime juices with the sugar and grenadine to dissolve the sugar. Place half of the chopped pineapple cubes in a 6-cup round ring mold or fluted tube cake pan. Pour in about 5 cups of the punch. Freeze until the punch is solid, at least overnight. Separately cover the remaining punch and pineapple cubes and refrigerate.

2. When ready to serve, stir in the rum and the remaining pineapple cubes. Pour into a punch bowl. Dip the outside of the ring mold in a large bowl of warm water until the frozen punch ring loosens from the mold, about 10 seconds. Un-mold the ice ring into the punch. Serve immediately.

A Mardi Gras Celebration Shopping List

Serves 10 to 12

Dairy

Unsalted butter (1¼ sticks)

Large eggs (4)

Freshly squeezed orange juice (3 cups)

Dried Herbs and Spices

Dried basil (1 tablespoon)

Ground hot red (cayenne) pepper (¼ teaspoon)

Ground cinnamon (1 teaspoon)

Garlic powder (1 teaspoon)

Nutmeg (1 teaspoon, preferably freshly grated)

Onion powder (1 teaspoon)

Sweet Hungarian paprika (2 tablespoons)

Dried thyme (1 tablespoon)

Fish

Large (21 to 25 count) shrimp (2 pounds)

Groceries

Baguette-shaped French bread (1 loaf)

Chicken broth, reduced-sodium (three 14½-ounce cans)

Pecans (1 cup coarsely chopped)

Crushed pineapple in juice (one 20-ounce can)

Unsweetened pineapple juice (3 cups)

Raisins (1 cup)

Canned red beans (two 15- to 19-ounce cans)

Long-grain rice, preferably converted (3 cups)

Colored decorating sugars, preferably yellow, green, and purple (1 jar of each)

Diced tomatoes in juice (one 28-ounce can)

Liquor

Bourbon (¼ cup)

Grenadine (¾ cup)

Dark or golden rum (1½ cups)

Dry white wine (2½ cups)

Meat

Andouille sausage or hot links (½ pound)

Boneless skinless chicken breasts (4 pounds)

Pantry Staples

Extra virgin olive oil (about ¾ cup)

Vegetable oil (1½ cups plus 2 tablespoons)

All-purpose flour (3 cups)

Confectioners' sugar (1 cup)

Granulated sugar (2 cups)

Superfine sugar (¾ cup)

Baking powder (1 tablespoon)

Hot red pepper sauce (to taste)

Produce

Celery (1 large head)

Eggplants (2 medium)

Garlic (1 head)

Green bell pepper (1 small)

Lemons (about 8, for 1½ cups fresh juice)

Limes (about 12, for 1½ cups fresh juice)

Yellow onions (1 small, 2 large)

Navel oranges (2, one for zest and both for
    ¼ cup juice for the cake)

Parsley (1 bunch)

Pineapple (1 ripe)

Red bell peppers (1 large, 1 small)

Scallions (7)

Shallots (7, for 1 cup chopped)

Yams (2 medium, for 1½ cups shredded)

Zucchini (2 medium)

A Mardi Gras Celebration Preparation Timetable

2 days ahead

Make ratatouille

1 day ahead

Make red bean dip; refrigerate

Bake sweet potato cake

Make punch; refrigerate

Make ice ring for punch; freeze

8 hours before serving

Make garlic crisps

4 hours before serving

Make étouffée; refrigerate

Just before guests arrive

Reheat dip

Place ice ring in punch

Just before serving

Make the shallot rice

Reheat étouffée

Reheat ratatouille

A Happy Birthday Buffet

My parents made sure that the birthday parties they gave for their growing sons were three very special days of the year. We were well aware of the effort and care that went into our parties. My mom was fa-

---

Serves 10

Baked Chicken with Chile-Yogurt Marinade

Couscous Salad with Saffron Vinaigrette

Romaine Hearts with Avocado, Grapefruit, and Red Onion

Warm Pita Bread*

Chocolate Sour Cream Cake

*Recipe not included

---

mous in the neighborhood for her arts-and-crafts approach to cake decoration. Her typical edible masterpieces were often trains, cars, and other vehicles, but her *pièce de résistance* was a record player complete with shiny black frosting to simulate the vinyl record. Dad would spend hours festooning the garage with crepe paper and other decorations to transform it into a proper party room. Whenever I give a birthday party, I still try to emulate the fun and excitement of those festivities.

There are a number of ways to approach a birthday party menu. One is to go with the celebrant's favorite foods. The only problem with this tactic is one person's favorite is another's not-so-favorite. I think it's better to go with a middle-of-the-road approach with recipes that everyone will enjoy, especially if the guest list is multigenerational.

For a main course that is sure to please almost every guest, chicken is always good, and chicken pieces are easiest to cook and eat. The zesty marinade blends many ingredients—yogurt, chiles, cilantro, and limes, among others—to give the baked chicken a mildly spicy lift that even conservative palates will enjoy. The starchy side dish is provided by a couscous salad, and greens are represented by a crisp romaine lettuce salad with avocados and grapefruit. I haven't suggested an appetizer for this menu because there are plenty of ideas in other chapters, from dips to classic hors d'oeuvres, so take your pick.

I don't think anyone has ever done a survey on favorite birthday cakes, but chocolate usually shows up high on most lists of dessert preferences. This is one of the easiest chocolate cakes imaginable, and one of the best. Just add the candles and get ready to sing a round of "Happy Birthday." And if you're wondering if my placement of this birthday menu in the New Year's section was arbitrary, it's not—I celebrate many birthdays in March, including my own.

Baked Chicken with Chile-Yogurt Marinade

Makes 10 servings

Make Ahead. The chicken can be marinated 8 hours ahead. The chicken is best served just after baking.

A platter of marinated chicken is always a popular buffet item, and I've been serving this at my parties for years. Choose cilantro, basil, or even parsley to fit your fancy or your guests' taste (I have cilantro-haters in my crowd, and you may, too). For the juiciest results, use bone-in, skin-on chicken. This marinade works well to protect skinless chicken from drying out—just reduce the baking time by a few minutes.

Chile-Yogurt Marinade

3 garlic cloves

1 jalapeño, halved lengthwise and seeded

1 large onion, cut into large chunks

¼ cup packed fresh cilantro, basil, or parsley leaves

One 16-ounce container plain low-fat yogurt

Grated zest of 2 limes

¼ cup fresh lime juice

2 tablespoons chili powder or pure ground mild chile, such as ancho

1 teaspoon salt

4 large (8 to 9 ounces each) chicken breast halves, each cut in half crosswise to make 8 pieces total

6 chicken drumsticks

6 chicken thighs

1. To make the marinade, with the machine running, drop the garlic and jalapeño through the feed tube of a food processor. Add the onion and cilantro, and pulse until the onion is finely chopped. Add the yogurt, lime zest and juice, chili powder, and salt, and process into a purée. (Or place all of the ingredients, but only 1 cup of the yogurt, in a blender and process until smooth. Transfer the marinade to a bowl and stir in the remaining yogurt.)

2. Divide the chicken pieces between two 1-gallon self-sealing plastic bags. Pour in the marinade and seal the bags. Refrigerate for at least 2 and up to 8 hours.

(continued)

3. Position two racks in the top third and center of the oven and preheat to 400°F. Line two large baking sheets with aluminum foil and lightly oil the foil. (This makes for easy cleanup.)

4. Remove the chicken from the marinade. Arrange on the baking sheets. Bake for 20 minutes. Turn the chicken and switch the positions of the baking sheets from top to bottom. Continue baking until a drumstick shows no sign of pink when pierced at the bone, about 25 minutes more. Transfer to a serving dish. Serve the chicken hot.

**Baked Ham with Pineapple
Chutney Glaze, page 14;
Yam and Yukon Gold
Potato Salad, page 18**

Jean's Flat Apple Pie, page 20; Five-Spice Hot Apple Cider, page 22

Blue-Ribbon Chili, page 31

Ohmigod! Brownies,
page 34

Chicken and Shrimp
Étouffée, page 42;
Shallot Rice, page 44

**Sweet Potato King Cake,
page 47**

Baked Chicken with Chile-Yogurt Marinade, page 55; Couscous Salad with Saffron Vinaigrette, page 57; Romaine Hearts with Avocado, Grapefruit, and Red Onion, page 59.

Chocolate Sour
Cream Cake,
page 60

Couscous Salad with Saffron Vinaigrette

Makes 10 servings
Make Ahead: The salad can be made up to 1 day ahead.

Two little steps make a big difference with this bright, attractive salad. First, take a minute to rub the clumps of couscous through your fingers before adding the vegetables and dressing. And, because the salad changes flavor as it absorbs the dressing, reserve some of the vinaigrette to add just before serving.

¾ cup plus 5 teaspoons olive oil, divided

1 teaspoon salt, divided, plus more to taste

2 cups (about 12 ounces) couscous

1 large red bell pepper, seeds and ribs removed, cut into ¼-inch dice

4 large carrots, peeled and cut into ¼-inch dice

4 scallions, white and green parts, chopped

¼ cup lemon juice

1 garlic clove, crushed through a press

½ teaspoon crumbled saffron

¼ teaspoon freshly ground black pepper, plus more to taste

⅛ teaspoon ground hot red (cayenne) pepper

2 tablespoons chopped fresh mint, plus more for garnish

1. Bring 2¼ cups water, 2 teaspoons olive oil, and ½ teaspoon of the salt to a boil in a medium saucepan over high heat. Stir in the couscous and remove from the heat. Cover tightly and let stand until the couscous is tender, about 5 minutes. Transfer the couscous to a large bowl. Fluff the couscous with a fork and cool completely. Using oiled fingers, rub the couscous to break up any clumps.

2. Heat 3 teaspoons (1 tablespoon) of the oil in a large skillet over medium heat. Add the red bell pepper and cook, stirring occasionally, until just tender, about 5 minutes. Transfer to a bowl and cool.

3. Bring a medium saucepan of lightly salted water to a boil over high heat. Add the carrots and cook until the color is a shade brighter and the carrots are crisp-

(continued)

tender, about 3 minutes. Drain, rinse under cold water, and drain well. Add to the couscous, with the the red bell pepper and scallions, and mix well.

4. Combine the lemon juice, garlic, saffron, remaining ½ teaspoon salt, black pepper, and cayenne in a blender. With the machine running, add the remaining olive oil. Pour half of the dressing over the couscous, add the mint, and mix well. Cover and refrigerate until chilled, at least 2 hours. (The salad can be made up to 1 day ahead, covered, and refrigerated.)

5. Just before serving, toss the salad with the remaining dressing and adjust the seasoning with salt and pepper. Transfer to a serving bowl and garnish with the mint. Serve chilled or at room temperature.

Romaine Hearts with Avocado, Grapefruit, and Red Onion

Makes 10 servings

Make Ahead: The dressing can be made up to 1 day ahead, covered, and refrigerated. The other salad components can be prepared up to 8 hours ahead, but the salad is best prepared right before serving.

This crisp salad has a mildly sweet dressing that accents the grapefruit. The avocados (tossed with a couple of tablespoons of the dressing), soaked and drained onions, and grapefruit sections can be prepared up to 8 hours ahead, stored in individual self-sealing plastic bags, and refrigerated. When it comes time to serve, it will only take a few minutes to toss it all together. If you use conventional romaine lettuce, it can be cleaned, wrapped in paper towels, and refrigerated in a large plastic bag for 8 hours.

Dressing

¼ cup red wine vinegar

2 tablespoons honey

½ teaspoon salt

½ teaspoon freshly ground black pepper

¾ cup vegetable oil

1 medium red onion, thinly sliced into half-moons

One 18-ounce package romaine lettuce hearts, rinsed, dried, and torn into bite-sized pieces

2 large grapefruits, peeled and cut into sections

3 ripe avocados, pitted, skinned, and cut into ¾-inch cubes

1. To make the dressing, place the vinegar, honey, salt, and pepper in a blender. With the machine running, add the oil and process to make a thick dressing.

2. Soak the onion in a bowl of cold water for 30 minutes to soften its sharpness. Drain well and pat dry with paper towels.

3. Just before serving, combine the lettuce, grapefruits, avocados, and onion in a large serving bowl. Add the dressing and toss. Serve immediately.

Chocolate Sour Cream Cake

Makes 12 servings

Make Ahead: The cake layers can be made up to 1 month ahead, wrapped in plastic wrap, and frozen. The completed cake can be made 1 day ahead.

This cake's simplicity is one of the many reasons I love it—you just mix up the batter (without creaming butter, separating eggs, or beating whites), pour into pans, and bake. And the frosting is pretty darned easy, too. It is best to use a supermarket brand of semisweet chocolate for the icing, as bittersweet can be a bit too bitter for the tangy sour cream—whisk in confectioners' sugar to taste to balance the tartness, if you wish. If you make the cake a day ahead, be sure to let it stand at room temperature at least 1 hour before serving to allow the butter in the batter to soften. Otherwise, you will serve hard, cold slabs of cake instead of tender, moist ones.

Cake

1 cup boiling water

8 tablespoons (1 stick) unsalted butter, cut up

3 ounces unsweetened chocolate, finely chopped

2 cups packed light brown sugar

2¼ cups all-purpose flour

1½ teaspoons baking soda

½ teaspoon salt

2 large eggs, at room temperature

½ cup sour cream, not reduced-fat, at room temperature

1 teaspoon vanilla extract

Frosting

12 ounces semisweet chocolate, finely chopped

1 cup sour cream, chilled

1 teaspoon vanilla extract

Store-bought icing in a tube, for inscribing

Fresh flowers, for decorating (optional, see Note)

1. To make the cake, position a rack in the center of the oven and preheat to 350°F. Lightly butter the insides of two 9-inch baking pans. Line the bottoms of the pans with rounds of wax paper. Dust the sides of the pans with flour, tapping out any excess.

2. Whisk the boiling water, butter, and chocolate in a large bowl until smooth. Using a handheld electric mixer on low speed, beat in the brown sugar, flour,

baking soda, and salt. Increase the speed to high and beat in the eggs, sour cream, and vanilla. Beat for 1 minute, scraping down the sides of the bowl often with a rubber spatula, until the batter is very smooth. Transfer to the pans and spread evenly.

3. Bake until a toothpick inserted in the center of the cake comes out clean, about 30 minutes. Transfer to wire cake racks and cool for 10 minutes. Run a knife around the insides of the cake pans to loosen the cakes. Invert and unmold the cakes onto the racks and remove the wax paper. Turn the cakes right side up and cool completely on the racks. (The cake layers can be made up to 1 month ahead, wrapped tightly in a double thickness of plastic wrap, and frozen. Defrost overnight before using.)

4. To make the frosting, melt the chocolate in the top part of a double boiler set over very hot, not simmering, water. Transfer the chocolate to a medium bowl and cool until tepid. Add the sour cream and vanilla. Whisk just until the frosting is smooth and forms soft peaks. (If the frosting is too soft to spread, place in a larger bowl of iced water. Let the frosting stand, whisking occasionally, until cooled and firm enough to spread.)

5. Place one cake layer upside-down into a serving platter. Slip 3 or 4 strips of wax paper under the circumference of the cake. Using a metal icing spatula, spread the layer with about ⅔ cup of the frosting. Top with the second layer, right side up. Slather the top and then the sides with the remaining frosting. Using the icing in the tube, inscribe the cake. Remove the wax paper strips. Refrigerate the cake to set the icing, about 15 minutes. (The cake can be made up to 1 day ahead, covered loosely with plastic wrap, and refrigerated. Remove the cake from the refrigerator 1 hour before serving.)

6. Just before serving, decorate the cake with the fresh flowers, if desired. Slice into wedges and serve.

(continued)

Note: If you wish to decorate beyond icing, nothing beats fresh flowers for simplicity and elegance. Just choose nontoxic, unsprayed blooms that are known to be edible. I often use gerberas (rinsed and patted dry to remove any insecticides, just in case), which are bright, large, and quite dramatic against the dark chocolate frosting. Roses from the garden are another fine choice. Some supermarkets carry edible flowers, which are usually small-bloomed varieties like pansies, violets, and nasturtiums. Use them if you wish, but frankly, you need a lot of them to make an impact. In either case, large or small, consider the flowers purely decorative because not many people actually enjoy eating flowers.

A Happy Birthday Buffet Shopping List

Serves 10

Dairy

Unsalted butter (1 stick)

Large eggs (2)

Sour cream, not reduced-fat (1½ cups)

Plain low-fat yogurt (one 16-ounce container)

Dried Herbs and Spices

Ground hot red (cayenne) pepper (⅛ teaspoon)

Chili powder or pure ground ancho chile
    (2 tablespoons)

Saffron threads (½ teaspoon)

Groceries

Semisweet chocolate (12 ounces)

Unsweetened chocolate (3 ounces)

Couscous (12 ounces)

Honey (2 tablespoons)

Icing for inscribing cake (1 tube)

Meat

4 large (8 to 9 ounces each) chicken breast
    halves

6 chicken drumsticks

6 chicken thighs

Miscellaneous

Fresh, nontoxic edible flowers for decorating
    cake (as needed, optional)

Pantry Staples

Olive oil (about 1 cup)

Vegetable oil (¾ cup)

Red wine vinegar (¼ cup)

All-purpose flour (2¼ cups)

Light brown sugar (2 cups)

Baking soda (1½ teaspoons)

Vanilla extract (2 teaspoons)

Produce

Hass avocados (3 ripe)

Carrots (4 large)

Cilantro (1 bunch)

Garlic (1 head)

Grapefruits (2 large)

Jalapeño (1)

Lemons (2 to make ¼ cup fresh juice)

Limes (2)

Mint (1 bunch)

Red bell pepper (1 large)

Romaine lettuce hearts (one 18-ounce package)

Red onion (1 medium)

Yellow onion (1 large)

Scallions (4)

A Happy Birthday Buffet Preparation Timetable

Up to 1 month ahead

    Make cake layers; freeze

1 day ahead

    Thaw and frost cake; refrigerate

    Make couscous salad; refrigerate

8 hours before serving

    Prepare dressing, onion, avocados, and grapefruits for romaine salad; refrigerate

    Marinate chicken

About 1 hour before serving

    Bake chicken; keep warm

    Remove cake from refrigerator

Just before serving

    Toss romaine salad

    Stir additional vinaigrette into couscous salad; adjust seasonings

    Decorate cake with flowers, if using

Part Two

Springtime
Celebrations

A Passover Seder

An Easter Dinner

A Spring Shower

A Mother's Day Brunch

A Passover Seder

Before I moved to Manhattan's Upper West Side, my experience with Jewish cuisine was limited to the occasional pastrami sandwich at a so-called New York deli in downtown San Francisco. My eyes were opened when I started frequenting *real* New York Jewish delicatessens *in situ*

Serves 8

Chicken Liver and Apple Spread

Salmon Gefilte Fish Terrine with Spicy Beet Salad

Beef Brisket with Red Wine Sauce

Potato and Leek Kugel

Roasted Carrot–Currant Haroset

Hazelnut Meringues with Fresh Berries

---

and enjoying homemade food in my friends' homes, usually at a Passover Seder or other holiday celebration.

It wasn't long before I learned how to make a mean chopped chicken liver spread, a brisket that any Jewish grandmother would be proud to serve, and other classics of the Jewish table. In fact, my brisket makes an annual showing at one friend's Seder, even if I can't be there myself—she drops by and picks it up on the way to her sister-in-law's. When my culinary students started asking me for recipes to spice up their Passover menus, I was happy to oblige with new creations. My education in this wonderful food was furthered immeasurably when I worked with Jeffrey Nathan (who is not only chef at Manhattan's Abigael's Restaurant but host of PBS-TV's "New Jewish Cuisine") on his cookbook, *Adventures in Jewish Cooking*. Cooking kosher is second nature to him, and he reviewed this menu to be sure that I hadn't accidentally broken any dietary laws.

The menu for this Seder updates the traditional foods. Apples are the secret ingredient to the moist chicken liver spread. Instead of poached gefilte fish balls, why not serve salmon terrine with a horseradish-spiked beet salad? Red wine gives backbone to the brisket sauce, which is not thickened with a roux or cornstarch, but by puréeing the seasoning vegetables with the cooking liquid. Leeks enhance the common potato kugel, and roasted carrots enliven haroset. Dessert is light—crisp hazelnut meringues filled with seasonal berries.

Even more than other meals for Judeo-Christian holidays, a Passover menu usually has lots of Make Ahead dishes. No eating is allowed until after the Seder ceremony, and the celebrants are too hungry to wait for the meal to cook. However, there is a lot of baking in this menu, and two ovens would help during preparation. If you have only one oven, stagger the cooking over a couple of days so you don't experience a jam-up.

Chicken Liver and Apple Spread

Makes about 3 cups, 8 to 10 servings
Make Ahead: The spread can be made up to 2 days ahead.

A bit of apple works wonders with this favorite appetizer. It keeps the spread from being too dry, a common problem because kosher dietary laws require the livers to be cooked until well done. Chicken fat (known as schmaltz in classic Jewish cooking terminology) does add extra richness and flavor, but if you don't have it handy, simply use vegetable oil and hold your head high.

2 tablespoons rendered chicken fat (see sidebar) or
    vegetable oil
1 large onion, chopped
1 Granny Smith apple, peeled, cored, and chopped into
    ½-inch cubes

1 teaspoon chopped fresh thyme, plus additional sprigs
    for garnish, or ½ teaspoon dried thyme
1 pound chicken livers, trimmed
2 large hard-cooked eggs, coarsely chopped
Kosher salt and freshly ground black pepper, to taste
Matzo, apple slices, and grapes, for serving

1. Heat the chicken fat or oil in a large nonstick skillet over medium heat. Add the onion and cook, stirring occasionally, until the onion is golden with brown edges, about 10 minutes. Add the apples. Cook with the lid partially covering the skillet, stirring occasionally, until the apples are tender and the onion is deep golden brown, about 10 minutes more. Stir in the thyme.

2. Meanwhile, position a broiler rack 6 inches from the source of heat and preheat the broiler. Lightly oil the broiler rack and spread the livers on the rack. Broil until the livers are browned, 4 to 5 minutes. Turn the livers and broil until the other side is brown and the livers are completely cooked through and show no sign of pink (use the tip of a knife to check), about 5 minutes more. Cool the livers completely.

3. Pulse the chicken livers, onion and apple mixture, and eggs in a food processor just until they are combined. Season with salt and pepper. Pack the spread into a serving bowl and cool completely. (The spread can be prepared up to 2 days ahead, covered, and refrigerated.)

4. Garnish the spread with thyme sprigs and serve with the matzo, apples, and grapes.

Chicken Fat

Some kosher butchers sell schmaltz (rendered chicken fat), but if you want the homemade kind, you'll have to think ahead. The next time you roast a chicken, simply collect the fat that is left in the roasting pan. Pour the fat out of the pan into a custard cup or another small bowl and let stand for 5 minutes. Skim off the clear yellow fat that rises to the surface (keep the dark juices for making a pan sauce for the chicken) and transfer to another custard cup. Refrigerate the fat until solid—overnight is best. Covered tightly, the schmaltz will keep for about 1 week, or freeze for up to 3 months.

Salmon Gefilte Fish Terrine with Spicy Beet Salad

Makes about 12 servings

Make Ahead: The terrine and beet salad can be made up to 1 day ahead.

Most gefilte fish is made with mild fish fillets such as whitefish and pike, which can be difficult to find outside of Jewish markets, even at Passover time. My students asked me to develop a gefilte fish recipe that used more readily available ingredients. And, they said, they wouldn't mind if they didn't have to poach balls of puréed fish, and the sugar that some families like in their gefilte fish would definitely be optional, if not omitted. Here is the delicious result, a baked salmon terrine that makes attractive pink slices. Served alongside, a shredded beet salad with horseradish vinaigrette takes the place of the traditional poached carrots.

Terrine

3 tablespoons olive oil, divided

½ cup finely chopped shallots

1 pound skinless salmon fillets, cut into 1-inch pieces

1 pound skinless flounder fillets, cut into 1-inch pieces

2 large eggs, beaten

¼ cup matzo meal

1 tablespoon sugar

1½ teaspoons kosher salt

½ teaspoon freshly ground black pepper

3 tablespoons chopped fresh dill

Beet Salad

5 medium beets, stems removed, peeled (see Note)

3 tablespoons prepared horseradish

1 tablespoon red wine vinegar

½ cup olive oil

2 scallions, white and green parts, chopped

Kosher salt, to taste

8 to 10 large Bibb lettuce leaves, for serving

1. Position a rack in the center of the oven and preheat to 350°F. Lightly oil an 8½ × 4½-inch glass loaf pan and line the bottom with wax paper.

2. To make the terrine, heat 1 tablespoon of the oil in a medium skillet over medium heat. Add the shallots and cook, stirring often, until softened, about 2 minutes. Scrape the shallots into a food processor. Add the salmon and flounder, and pulse until coarsely chopped. Add the eggs, matzo meal, remaining 2 tablespoons oil, sugar, salt, and pepper. With the machine running, slowly add

¾ cup water and process until it has been absorbed by the fish mixture. Add the dill and pulse just until combined. Spread evenly in the loaf pan. Place a piece of oiled wax paper, oiled side down, on top of the salmon mixture.

3. Place the loaf pan in a larger roasting pan. Place the roasting pan in the oven. Slide out the rack, pour in enough hot water to come ½ inch up the sides of the loaf pan, and carefully slide the rack back into the oven. Bake until an instant-read thermometer inserted in the center of the pan reads 160°F, about 1¼ hours. Transfer the loaf pan to a wire rack and cool completely.

4. Remove the top piece of wax paper. Invert the terrine onto a large piece of plastic wrap and remove bottom piece of wax paper. Wrap tightly in the plastic wrap and refrigerate until chilled, at least 3 hours or overnight. (The terrine can be made up to 1 day ahead.)

5. To make the salad, shred the beets in a food processor or on a box grater. In a medium bowl, whisk the horseradish and vinegar. Gradually whisk in the oil. Add the beets and scallions and mix well. Season with the salt. Cover and refrigerate until chilled, at least 1 hour. (The beet salad can be made up to 1 day ahead.)

6. To serve, slice the terrine crosswise into ½-inch thick slices. For each serving, place a lettuce leaf on each salad plate, top with a slice of the terrine, and add a portion of the salad to one side. Serve cold.

Note: Always wear an apron when preparing beets, as beet juice is a notorious clothes-stainer. To help keep the juice from staining your skin, rub your hands with a little vegetable or olive oil before peeling the beets.

Beef Brisket with Red Wine Sauce

Makes 8 to 10 servings
Make Ahead: The brisket can be prepared up to 1 day ahead.

I never had brisket until I moved to New York, and now it is one of my favorite cuts, delivering lots of beefy flavor and a melt-in-your-mouth texture that you can't get from a steak. To avoid using a butter-based roux (dairy) or cornstarch (not kosher for Passover), the delectable sauce for this dish is thickened by puréeing the vegetables in the braising liquid. I haven't found a canned beef broth (kosher or not) that I really like, nor am I a fan of bouillon cubes. If you have homemade beef stock in the freezer, use it or substitute a good canned chicken broth. This makes plenty of sauce, but it will come in handy to serve with the kugel and any leftover brisket.

6 pounds beef brisket, trimmed

Kosher salt and freshly ground black pepper, to taste

2 tablespoons vegetable oil

1 large onion, chopped

1 large celery rib, chopped

1 large carrot, peeled and chopped

1 large baking potato, peeled and cut into 1-inch chunks

8 garlic cloves, peeled

2 cups hearty red wine, such as Cabernet Sauvignon

2 tablespoons tomato paste

6 cups homemade beef stock or canned chicken broth

4 teaspoons chopped fresh thyme or 2 teaspoons dried thyme

1 bay leaf

Fresh thyme sprigs, for garnish (optional)

1. Position a rack in the center of the oven and preheat the oven to 325°F.

2. Season the brisket with the salt and pepper. Heat the oil in a large Dutch oven or flameproof casserole over medium-high heat. Add the brisket and cook until the underside is browned, about 3 minutes. Turn and brown the other side, about 3 minutes more. Transfer to a large platter.

3. Add the onion, celery, and carrot to the fat in the pot, and cover. Cook, stirring occasionally, until the vegetables soften, about 5 minutes. Stir in the potato and garlic, and cook for 1 minute. Add the wine and tomato paste and bring to

a boil, scraping up the browned bits in the bottom of the pan with a wooden spoon. Return the brisket and any juices to the Dutch oven. Add the stock, thyme, and bay leaf. Do not worry if it doesn't completely cover the brisket, as the brisket will shrink during cooking. Return the liquid to a boil. Cover tightly.

4. Place in the oven and bake, occasionally turning the brisket in the juices, until the brisket is very tender, about 2½ hours. (The brisket can be prepared to this point 1 day ahead. Cool the brisket and vegetables in the cooking liquid. Cover and refrigerate. When ready to serve, scrape off any hardened fat from the surface of the chilled cooking liquid. Cover and reheat the brisket and vegetables in the Dutch oven over medium heat until the juices are simmering and the brisket is heated through, about 25 minutes.)

5. Transfer the brisket to a platter, cover loosely with aluminum foil, and let stand while making the sauce. Let the cooking juices and vegetables cool for 5 minutes, then skim off any fat that rises to the surface. Discard the bay leaf. Using a slotted spoon, transfer the vegetables in the pot to a blender or food processor. Purée the vegetables, adding as much as 3 cups of the cooking liquid through the feed tube to make the sauce—adjust the amount of liquid to make the sauce as thick as you like. (Save and freeze any remaining cooking liquid to use as beef broth in another recipe, or discard.) Season the sauce with salt and pepper.

6. Slice the brisket across the grain. Arrange overlapping layers of the sliced brisket on a large deep platter. Ladle about 1 cup of the sauce over the sliced brisket. Garnish the brisket with a few fresh thyme sprigs, if you wish. Serve hot, with the sauce passed on the side.

Potato and Leek Kugel

Makes 8 to 10 servings

Make Ahead: The kugel can be prepared up to 8 hours ahead.

Potato kugel is a classic Jewish holiday side dish . . . some would say that it could use a makeover. The leeks add an elegance that befits a special holiday.

6 tablespoons olive oil, divided

3 cups chopped leeks, white and pale green parts, well rinsed and drained

4 pounds baking potatoes, peeled

1½ teaspoons kosher salt

6 large eggs, beaten

¼ cup plus 3 tablespoons matzo meal, divided

½ teaspoon freshly ground black pepper

2 tablespoons chopped fresh parsley, for serving

1. Position a rack in the center of the oven and preheat to 375°F. Generously oil the inside of a 13 × 9-inch baking dish with 2 tablespoons of the oil.

2. Heat 2 tablespoons oil in a large skillet over medium heat. Add the leeks and cook, stirring often, until softened, about 8 minutes.

3. Using a food processor or the large holes of a box grater, shred the potatoes and place in a large bowl. Stir in the salt. Let stand for 5 minutes, then drain well in a colander. Return to the bowl and mix in the leeks, eggs, ¼ cup matzo meal, and the pepper. Spread evenly in the prepared baking dish and sprinkle with the remaining 3 tablespoons matzo meal. Drizzle with the remaining 2 tablespoons oil. Cover tightly with aluminum foil.

4. Bake for 45 minutes. Uncover and bake until the top is golden and the vegetables are tender, about 45 minutes more. (The kugel can be made 8 hours ahead, cooled, and covered with aluminum foil. Reheat in a 400°F oven until heated through, about 15 minutes. Remove the foil and cook for another 5 minutes to crisp the topping.)

5. Sprinkle with the parsley. Cut into squares and serve hot.

Roasted Carrot—Currant Haroset

Makes about 6 cups; 10 to 12 servings
Make Ahead: The haroset can be made up to 3 days ahead.

Symbolizing the mortar used by the Hebrew slaves in Egypt, this chunky condiment is an essential part of the Seder ceremony. However, it often stays on the table for the entire meal, so it needs to be delicious as well as symbolic. Roasted carrots, like the more usual raw apples, are naturally sweet, and make a fine foundation for other traditional haroset ingredients like dried fruits and nuts.

1 pound carrots, peeled and cut into 2-inch lengths

1 teaspoon vegetable oil

1 cup finely chopped pecans

⅔ cup dried currants

¼ cup port or sweet red wine, as needed

2 tablespoons honey

1 teaspoon ground cinnamon

1 teaspoon ground ginger

1. Position a rack in the upper third of the oven and preheat to 425°F.

2. Toss the carrots and the oil in a 13 × 9-inch metal baking dish. Add ¼ cup water. Cover tightly with aluminium foil. Bake for 30 minutes. Uncover and bake until the carrots are lightly browned and tender, about 20 minutes more. Cool completely.

3. Coarsely chop the carrots, transfer to a medium bowl, and mash with a large fork until chunky. Add the pecans, currants, ¼ cup port, honey, cinnamon, and ginger, and mix well with a large fork. The haroset should remain chunky, but be smooth enough to spread, so add more port if needed. Let stand for at least 1 hour before serving to blend the flavors. (The haroset can be made up to 3 days ahead, covered, and refrigerated. Bring to room temperature before serving.)

Hazelnut Meringues with Fresh Berries

Makes 8 servings

Make Ahead: The meringues can be made up to 3 days ahead.

These crunchy treats are based on a recipe from my friend David Lebovitz, one of America's great bakers. His meringues are baked at a very low temperature, so allow at least 3 hours for them to dry properly. In fact, if you have the time, they will benefit from an overnight stay in the turned-off oven. Do not try to make or store meringues during rainy or humid weather, or they will stay stubbornly sticky.

Hazelnut Meringues

½ cup chopped hazelnuts (see Note)

½ cup confectioners' sugar

6 large egg whites, at room temperature

⅛ teaspoon cream of tartar

1 cup granulated sugar

¼ teaspoon almond extract

Filling

2 quarts fresh strawberries, hulled and thinly sliced

¼ cup granulated sugar

1 tablespoon lemon juice

Mint sprigs, for garnish

1. Position racks in the center and top third of the oven and preheat to 225°F. Line two baking sheets with parchment paper or silicone baking pads.

2. Process the hazelnuts and confectioners' sugar in a food processor until the hazelnuts are finely ground into a powder. Beat the egg whites and cream of tartar with an electric mixer on low speed until the whites are foamy. Increase the speed to high and beat until the whites form soft peaks. Still beating, add the granulated sugar, 1 tablespoon at a time, until the whites are shiny and firm. Using a large rubber spatula, fold in the ground hazelnuts just until incorporated.

3. Using about ¾ cup for each meringue, drop the mixture in mounds on the lined baking sheets, spacing them about 2 inches apart. Using the back of a large, wet spoon, spread each mound into a 4-inch wide round and make an indentation in the center to form a shell.

4. Bake until the meringues are crisp and pale beige, 2½ to 3 hours. Cool for 10 minutes on the pan. (For extra-crisp meringues, turn off the oven, and let the meringues stand in the turned-off oven overnight.) Carefully peel the meringues from the paper. (The meringues can be made 3 days ahead and stored in an airtight container at room temperature.)

5. Meanwhile, to make the filling, combine the strawberries, sugar, and lemon juice in a medium bowl. Cover and refrigerate for at least 1 and up to 8 hours.

6. To serve, place a meringue on each plate. Using a slotted spoon, fill each meringue with the berries. Spoon some of the berry juices around each meringue. Garnish with the mint sprigs and serve.

Note: Many supermarkets carry chopped hazelnuts in the baking supplies section. These hazelnuts have not been peeled, but they work perfectly well in this recipe. If you want to use toasted and peeled hazelnuts, see the instructions on page 235.

A Passover Seder Shopping List

Serves 8

Dairy/Refrigerated

Large eggs (16)

Prepared horseradish (3 tablespoons)

Dried Herbs and Spices

(Dried basil (2 teaspoons)

Bay leaf (1)

Ground cinnamon (1 teaspoon)

Ground ginger (1 teaspoon)

Dried thyme (2½ teaspoons, if not using fresh
    thyme)

Fish

Flounder fillets, skinless (1 pound)

Salmon fillets, skinless (1 pound)

Groceries

Almond extract (¼ teaspoon)

Chicken broth, reduced-sodium canned (6 cups,
    if not using homemade beef stock)

Dried currants (⅔ cup)

Honey (2 tablespoons)

Chopped hazelnuts (½ cup)

Matzo meal (about ⅔ cup)

Matzo sheets (as needed, for serving chicken
    liver spread)

Pecans (1 cup)

Tomato paste (2 tablespoons)

Liquor

Port wine or sweet red wine (about ¼ cup)

Hearty dry red wine (2 cups)

Meat

Beef brisket (6 pounds)

Chicken livers (1 pound)

Miscellaneous

Beef stock, homemade (6 cups, or use canned
    chicken broth)

Rendered chicken fat (2 tablespoons, optional)

Pantry staples

Confectioners' sugar (½ cup)

Granulated sugar (1⅓ cups)

Cream of tartar (⅛ teaspoon)

Olive oil (¾ cup)

Vegetable oil (about ½ cup, slightly less if
    using chicken fat for the spread)

Red wine vinegar (1 tablespoon)

Produce

Granny Smith apples (1, plus as needed for serving chicken liver spread)

Beets (5 medium)

Bibb lettuce (2, for 8 large leaves)

Carrots (1 pound, plus 1 large)

Celery (1 large rib)

Fresh dill (1 bunch)

Garlic (1 head)

Grapes (1 bunch, to serve with chicken liver spread)

Leeks (4 to 5 medium, to make 3 cups chopped white and pale green parts)

Lemons (1)

Yellow onions (2 large, 2 medium)

Fresh parsley (1 bunch)

Baking potatoes (4 pounds plus 1 large)

Scallions (2)

Shallots (about 4 large, for $\frac{1}{2}$ cup finely chopped)

Strawberries (2 quarts)

Fresh thyme (2 bunches)

Yams (2 pounds)

A Passover Seder Preparation Timetable

3 days ahead

Make haroset; refrigerate

Make meringues; store airtight at room temperature

2 days ahead

Make chicken liver spread; refrigerate

1 day ahead

Make salmon terrine; refrigerate

Make beet salad; refrigerate

Make beef brisket; refrigerate

8 hours before serving

Make potato kugel; refrigerate

Prepare berries for meringues; refrigerate

Just before serving

Slice terrine; arrange on lettuce

Reheat kugel

Reheat brisket; make sauce

An Easter Dinner

When Easter comes around, I am like a racehorse let out of the gate. It's been a few months since the last proper holiday dinner, and I pull out all of the stops to make this meal a particularly memorable one. I go out of my way

---

Serves 8

Deviled Eggs with Fresh Horseradish

Asparagus, Potato, and Leek Soup

Roast Leg of Lamb with Herbs

Roasted Lemon Potatoes with Artichokes

Green Beans with Feta and Olives

Angel Food Cake with Lemon Mousse Frosting

---

for the longest tulips and tallest lilies for the floral arrangement, and search for special favors to dress up the dining room.

Even when there are only adults at the table, I still use this holiday as an excuse to ply my guests with jelly beans (spice flavored, not fruit, for me, please), chocolate-covered marshmallow eggs, malted milk eggs, and of course, yellow marshmallow chicks. A trip to the local discount merchandise emporium always yields a treasure trove of inexpensive mini-straw baskets, ready to fill up with goodies. For place cards, you can write the guests' names with indelible ink on decorated eggs and tuck them into the baskets with some colorful excelsior. If you don't have time to dip eggs, simply hard-cook brown eggs and write the names on those with colored pens. One year, a discount store had small, bargain-priced plush animals that I sat up at each place setting. The table looked especially inviting that year, with all of the bunnies sitting at attention.

Easter, like all holidays, comes with its own set of special foods. The egg, naturally, is the most important of these traditional ingredients, and lamb, spring vegetables such as asparagus and artichokes, and seasonings of fresh herbs and horseradish also find their way into this springtime menu. I have Greek Orthodox friends who often invite me to their Easter dinner, which includes lamb, lemon potatoes, and green beans. Their influence rubbed off on me. This menu has a slight Greek flavor, as a result.

I like serving soup as the first course at sit-down dinners because it gives the cook a breather before the last-minute preparations for the main course and side dishes. For this menu, I serve the asparagus soup about 15 minutes before the roast is done. When the soup dishes are cleared, it's just about time to take the lamb and potatoes out of the oven. As the roast rests, the green beans can be quickly sautéed. Try this timing trick, and I bet you'll consider soup often as the appetizer for formal dinner menus.

Deviled Eggs with Fresh Horseradish

Makes 16 appetizers
Make Ahead: The eggs can be prepared 1 day ahead.

My goal was to make deviled eggs that even I would like (deviled eggs being high on the list of foods that I usually say "no thanks" to). The result, made zesty with fresh horseradish, is a remarkably fresh version of a stodgy classic. Don't make these with bottled horseradish, as its vinegar won't do a thing for the eggs. And while you may have your own method of boiling eggs, try the method here, which prevents cracking and discolored yolks.

8 large eggs

¼ cup mayonnaise

2 tablespoons freshly grated horseradish (see Note),
   plus more for garnish

1 tablespoon heavy cream, half-and-half, or milk

Salt and freshly ground black pepper, to taste

Chopped fresh parsley leaves or chives, for garnish

1. Place the eggs in a medium saucepan and add enough cold water to cover. Bring just to a boil over high heat. Remove the saucepan from the heat and cover tightly. Let stand for 12 minutes.

2. Pour out the hot water from the saucepan and replace it with ice water. Let the eggs stand until chilled, about 10 minutes. Crack the eggs. Starting at the largest end, and working under a thin stream of cold running water, remove the egg shells.

3. Cut each egg in half lengthwise and remove the yolks. Using a rubber spatula, rub the yolks through a wire sieve into a small bowl. Stir in the mayonnaise, horseradish, and cream, and season with salt and pepper. Use a small spoon to stuff the egg whites with the filling. (For a more professional look, transfer the yolk mixture to a pastry bag fitted with a ½-inch wide star tip. Pipe the yolk mixture back into the whites. This may sound fussy, but actually it is a lot easier and better-looking than spooning the filling into the whites.) Place on a serving plat-

ter, cover loosely with plastic wrap, and refrigerate until serving, up to 8 hours.
4. To serve, grate a little more horseradish on top of each egg and sprinkle with parsley. (I often grate horseradish and sprinkle parsley all over the platter as an additional garnish.) Serve chilled.

Note: You'll find fresh horseradish root at most produce stores in the spring. Pare away the thick black peel with a sharp knife, and grate the white flesh with a microplane zester with moderately large holes or on the small holes of a box grater. Purchase a 4- to 6-inch length of horseradish root; you will not use all of it, but it can be preserved for another use (add it to mayonnaise or mustard to add distinction to these condiments). Grate the leftover root and place in a small covered jar. Pour in enough cider or white vinegar to cover the root. Refrigerated, the horseradish will keep for a couple of months.

Asparagus, Potato, and Leek Soup

Makes 8 servings

Make Ahead: The soup can be made 1 day ahead, cooled, covered, and refrigerated. Reheat gently over low heat, adding more stock to thin it to the desired consistency.

This lovely soup, with the very harmonious trio of asparagus, leeks, and potato, is the perfect soup for an Easter dinner. For a really elegant garnish, randomly drizzle a teaspoon or so of (room temperature) heavy cream over each serving. If Easter comes late and the weather is warm, chill the soup and serve it as "Asparagus Vichyssoise."

3 pounds asparagus

3 tablespoons unsalted butter

2 cups chopped and well-rinsed leeks (white and pale
    green parts only), about 4 medium

One 48-ounce can reduced-sodium chicken broth

1 large (about 10 ounces) baking potato, such as russet
    or Burbank, peeled and cut into 1-inch dice

½ cup heavy cream

Salt and freshly ground black pepper, to taste

Additional heavy cream for garnish, optional

1. Rinse the asparagus well. Bend back each stalk, letting the asparagus snap naturally where the tender flesh becomes tough and woody. Discard the woody stems. Cut off the tips from about one third of the asparagus and reserve for the garnish. Cut the remaining asparagus into 1-inch pieces.

2. Melt the butter in a large saucepan over medium-low heat. Add the leeks and cover. Cook, occasionally uncovering to stir the leeks, until the leeks are tender, about 10 minutes.

3. Add the broth, chopped asparagus, and the potato, and bring to a boil over high heat. Return the heat to medium-low and simmer, partially covered, until the potatoes are very tender, about 30 minutes. Stir in the heavy cream and season with salt and pepper.

4. Meanwhile, bring a medium saucepan of lightly salted water to a boil over

high heat. Add the reserved asparagus tips and cook until barely tender, about 4 minutes. Drain, rinse under cold water, and drain again.

5. In batches, purée the soup in a blender (or use a handheld blender to purée the soup in the pot). Return the soup to the pot and add the asparagus tips. Cook through, stirring often, until the tips are heated and the soup is piping hot. (The soup can be prepared up to 1 day ahead, cooled, covered, and refrigerated. Reheat gently over low heat, stirring often. If the reheated soup seems too thick, add additional broth to thin it as needed.)

6. Transfer the soup to a warmed soup tureen and serve hot, drizzling each serving with a few drops of heavy cream, if desired.

Roast Leg of Lamb with Herbs

Makes 8 servings

Make Ahead: The lamb and stock can be prepared up to 1 day ahead.

Here's one of the easiest, and best, ways I know to roast a boneless leg of lamb. Have the butcher bone and butterfly the lamb, and make a stock from the bones for the sauce. (Alternatively, buy a 4-pound boned and butterflied leg of lamb and 1½ pounds lamb neck.) Unfortunately, the amount of bones won't make the richest stock, so it's necessary to sneak in beef broth to add flavor—if you use canned broth, no one will know. The lamb itself will only take about 30 minutes to roast to rosy-pink perfection, each slice accented with mustard, garlic, and herbs.

One 6¼-pound leg of lamb, boned and butterflied by the butcher, bones reserved and sawed into 2-inch pieces

½ teaspoon salt

¼ teaspoon freshly ground black pepper

1 tablespoon vegetable oil

One 14½-ounce can reduced-sodium beef broth, or 1¾ cups homemade beef stock

2 tablespoons Dijon mustard

1 garlic clove, crushed through a press

2 tablespoons chopped fresh rosemary

1 tablespoons chopped fresh thyme

1. The night before cooking, using a sharp, thin knife, trim the lamb of excess fat and any thin membrane. Season the lamb with the salt and pepper. Wrap in plastic wrap and refrigerate overnight.

2. To make lamb stock, heat the oil in a medium saucepan over high heat. Add the lamb bones and cook, turning occasionally, until well browned. Add the beef broth and enough cold water to cover the bones by 1 inch, about 1 quart. Bring to a boil, skimming off any foam that rises to the surface. Reduce the heat to low. Simmer for at least 2 and up to 4 hours. Strain and let stand for 10 minutes. Skim off any fat that rises to the surface. (The stock can be made 1 day ahead, cooled, covered, and refrigerated.)

3. Position a rack in the top third of the oven and preheat to 450°F.   *(continued)*

4. Place the lamb, smooth side up, on a large, heavy rimmed baking sheet, such as a half-sheet pan, or in a shallow roasting pan. Mix the mustard and garlic. Spread the lamb with the garlic mustard. Sprinkle the rosemary and thyme over the lamb. Roast the lamb until an instant-read thermometer inserted in a thick part of the lamb reads 125°F for medium-rare, about 25 minutes. Transfer the lamb to a carving board and let stand for 10 minutes.

5. Meanwhile, place the baking sheet with any cooking juices over two burners on high heat. Add 2 cups of the lamb stock (reserve the remaining stock for another purpose) and bring to a boil, scraping up the browned bits in the pan with a wooden spatula. Boil until the stock is reduced to 1 cup. Season with salt and pepper.

6. Using a sharp, thin knife, slice the meat across the grain and transfer to a serving platter. Pour any carving juices and the pan sauce over the meat. Serve immediately.

Salmon Gefilte Fish
Terrine with Spicy
Beet Salad, page 70

Hazelnut
Meringues with
Fresh Berries,
page 76

Asparagus, Potato, and
Leek Soup, page 85

Roast Leg of Lamb with Herbs, page 87; Roasted Lemon Potatoes with Artichokes, page 89; Green Beans with Feta and Olives, page 90

Smoked Salmon and
Watercress Sandwiches,
page 97

Jackie O's, page 104

Baked Mascarpone-Stuffed
French Toast, page 109;
Berry-Maple Compote, page 111;
Mimosa Sunrise, page 113

Cedar-Smoked Salmon with
Cucumber Salsa, page 120

Grilled Pineapple Sundaes with Caramel Rum Sauce, page 124

Roasted Lemon Potatoes with Artichokes

Makes 8 servings

Make Ahead: The potatoes are best prepared just before serving.

This Greek-inspired recipe can be baked in the same oven as the lamb. Start the potatoes about 1 hour before serving.

4 large baking potatoes, peeled and cut lengthwise into
    sixths

3 tablespoons extra virgin olive oil, divided

Two 10-ounce packages frozen artichoke hearts, thawed

Grated zest of 2 lemons

3 tablespoons lemon juice

2 tablespoons chopped fresh parsley

Salt and freshly ground black pepper, to taste

1. Position a rack in the lower third of the oven and preheat to 450°F. Lightly oil a large, rimmed baking sheet or shallow baking pan.

2. Toss the potatoes with 2 tablespoons of the oil in a large bowl. Spread on the baking sheet. Bake for 15 minutes. Turn the potatoes with a metal spatula and bake for 15 minutes more. Toss the artichokes with the remaining 1 tablespoon olive oil and mix into the potatoes. Continue baking until the vegetables are tender and lightly browned, about 20 minutes more. Transfer the potatoes and artichokes to a large bowl. Cover with aluminum foil to keep warm, if necessary (you may need to do this while cooking the green beans in this menu).

3. Sprinkle with the lemon zest, then the lemon juice and parsley. Season with the salt and pepper. Transfer to a serving dish and serve hot.

Green Beans with Feta and Olives

Makes 8 servings

Make Ahead: The green beans can be prepared 1 day ahead. Cook them with the other ingredients just before serving.

This combination of green beans, olives, and feta cheese tastes like a trip to a Greek island. I prefer French or Bulgarian feta, which is creamier than other kinds.

1¼ pounds green beans, trimmed and cut into 2-inch lengths

2 tablespoons extra virgin olive oil

3 tablespoons chopped shallots

½ cup pitted and coarsely chopped black Mediterranean olives, such as Kalamata

Salt and freshly ground black pepper, to taste

½ cup (2 ounces) feta cheese, crumbled

1. Bring a large pot of lightly salted water to a boil over high heat. Add the green beans and cook, uncovered, until the beans are crisp-tender, about 5 minutes. Drain and rinse under cold water. Drain well. (The green beans can be prepared up to 1 day ahead. Pat the green beans dry with paper towels. Wrap in more paper towels and store in self-sealing plastic bags in the refrigerator.)

2. Heat the oil in a large skillet over medium-high heat. Add the shallots and cook, stirring often, until softened, about 1 minute. Add the green beans and olives and cook, stirring often, until the green beans are hot, about 5 minutes. Season with salt and pepper

3. Transfer to a serving dish and sprinkle the cheese on top. Serve immediately.

Angel Food Cake with Lemon Mousse Frosting

Makes 12 servings

Make Ahead: The cake can be made 1 day ahead. Frost the cake up to 8 hours before serving.

Recently, after an especially busy day of recipe testing, I found myself with a bowl of lemon mousse and an unfrosted angel food cake. I was delighted to find that the mousse also made a fine frosting, and a dessert was born. Angel food cakes are simple to make, if you have the right pan. Avoid nonstick angel food pans—the batter needs a metal surface in order to climb up the sides properly. Angel food cakes are always cooled upside down, so the pans have little feet on the edges or an elongated center tube to keep the cake itself from touching the surface. If necessary, elevate the cake pan by balancing the edges of the pan on 3 coffee mugs of the same height. If you wish, serve sliced strawberries alongside the cake.

1 cup cake flour (not self-rising)

½ cup confectioners' sugar

12 large egg whites, at cool room temperature (see
  Note)

1 teaspoon cream of tartar

1⅓ cups granulated sugar

1½ teaspoons vanilla extract

Grated zest of 2 lemons

Lemon Mousse Frosting (page 160)

1. Position a rack in the center of the oven and preheat to 350°F.

2. Sift the cake flour and confectioners' sugar together. Whip the egg whites in a large bowl with an electric mixer on low speed until foamy. Add the cream of tartar and increase the speed to high. Whip until the whites form soft peaks. Add the granulated sugar, 2 tablespoons at a time, whipping until the whites are stiff and shiny. Beat in the vanilla and lemon zest. In two additions, sift the flour mixture over the whites and fold it in with a large rubber spatula. Scrape the batter into an ungreased aluminum (not nonstick) angel food cake pan.

3. Bake until the cake is golden brown and the top springs back when lightly pressed, about 40 minutes. Invert the cake pan onto a heatproof surface and

let the cake cool, upside down. (The cake can be prepared up to 1 day ahead, covered with a cake dome at room temperature. Do not wrap in plastic wrap, which could make the cake sticky.)

4. Run a long knife around the inside of the pan to release the cake. Remove the cake from the pan, gently pulling it away from the base and tube. Place the cake on a serving platter. Frost the top and sides of the cake with the lemon mousse. Refrigerate until ready to serve. (The frosted cake can be refrigerated for up to 8 hours.)

Note: **Be sure to reserve 6 yolks for the frosting.**

An Easter Dinner Shopping List

Serves 8

Dairy

Unsalted butter (1 stick plus 3 tablespoons)

Feta cheese (½ cup crumbled, 2 ounces)

Heavy cream (about 1½ cups)

Large eggs (2 dozen total; 8 whole eggs for
  deviled eggs, plus 12 egg whites for the
  cake and 6 yolks for the mousse frosting)

Frozen

Artichoke hearts (two 10-ounce packages)

Groceries

Beef broth, reduced-sodium (one 14½-ounce
  can, or use 2 cups homemade beef stock)

Chicken broth, reduced-sodium (one 48-ounce
  can)

Cake flour (1 cup)

Mayonnaise (¼ cup)

Mediterranean black olives, such as Kalamata
  (½ cup pitted)

Meat

Leg of lamb (one 6¼-pound leg, boned, bones
  reserved and sawed into 2-inch pieces)

Pantry Staples

Dijon mustard (2 tablespoons)

Extra virgin olive oil (5 tablespoons)

Vegetable oil (1 tablespoon)

Confectioners' sugar (1¼ cups)

Granulated sugar (1⅓ cups)

Cornstarch (2 teaspoons)

Cream of tartar (1 teaspoon)

Vanilla extract (1½ teaspoons)

Produce

Asparagus (3 pounds)

Garlic (1 head)

Green beans (1¼ pounds)

Horseradish (one 4- to 6-inch long root)

Leeks (4 medium)

Lemons (8)

Parsley (1 bunch)

Baking potatoes (5 large)

Rosemary (1 bunch)

Shallots (2 medium, for 3 tablespoons
  chopped)

Thyme (1 bunch)

An Easter Dinner Preparation Timetable

1 day ahead

Make the deviled eggs; refrigerate

Prepare lamb; refrigerate

Make lamb stock; refrigerate

Make asparagus soup; refrigerate

Blanch green beans; refrigerate

Bake cake; wrap in plastic, and store at room temperature

Make lemon mousse icing

8 hours before serving

Frost cake; refrigerate

Peel potatoes; cut and store in cold water

1 hour before serving

Roast potatoes on lower rack

45 minutes before serving

Roast lamb on upper rack

Just before serving

Reheat soup

Make sauce while roasted lamb rests

Make green beans

Finish potatoes

A Spring Shower

Just as it has for many other social events, the etiquette of the bridal shower has evolved. When I was growing up in the fifties and sixties, showers were strictly "ladies only," and they carried a potent amount of feminine mystique. I

Serves 8

Smoked Salmon and Watercress Sandwiches

Chicken Cutlets in Wild Mushroom—Marsala Sauce

Bow-Tie Pasta with Snow Peas and Dill

Glazed Baby Carrots with Currants

Strawberry-Almond Ice Cream Cake

Jackie O's

---

can clearly remember the phalanx of female relatives sitting in rows in our living room, and the pairs of immaculate gloves clutching shiny purses. Occasionally, I would catch a glimpse of an embarrassed bride-to-be wearing a ribbon-festooned paper plate. It seemed natural that she was embarrassed, as it all looked pretty silly to me. What did I know? A bridal shower is a rite of passage right up there with the wedding itself.

Now, a bridal or baby shower can easily accommodate both sexes, and the atmosphere is more like a generic party. Today's showers don't just celebrate the bride, but the bridal couple. On the other hand, I have many women friends who are perfectly happy to have an afternoon or evening out without their mates in tow. And, according to an informal and totally unscientific survey I did on the subject, the majority of showers are still steeped in tradition and considered to be off-limits to men. (I was surprised to hear how many young women friends of mine were disappointed when the friends at their showers did *not* make a paper-plate "shower hat." So, when devising this menu, I couldn't help but think of the kind of food that would appeal to a large group of women of varying ages. There's no reason why this should be a springtime shower, except that as long as the June wedding remains so popular, showers will continue to be held in April or May.

The menu starts with delicate smoked salmon sandwiches, then segues into a main course of chicken in a marsala-mushroom sauce. The challenge in cooking boneless, skinless chicken is keeping it moist without overcooking it, and this recipe is prepared in steps that help to avoid this dilemma. Ice cream cake is the perfect Make Ahead dessert. And, as befits an especially festive occasion, serve a special drink, like the fruit-juice-and-vodka Jackie O cocktails offered here.

Smoked Salmon and Watercress Sandwiches

Makes 32 bite-sized sandwiches, 8 to 12 servings
Make Ahead: The sandwiches can be made 1 day ahead.

These classy little sandwiches are a snap to make. Chop the watercress leaves by hand, not in a food processor, or they'll give off chlorophyll and give a green tint to the pink butter.

4 ounces sliced smoked salmon

8 tablespoons (1 stick) unsalted butter, at room
temperature

¼ cup finely chopped watercress leaves

Freshly ground black pepper, to taste

16 slices thin-sliced white sandwich bread

Watercress sprigs, for garnish

1. Pulse the smoked salmon in a food processor until it is finely chopped. Add the butter and process, scraping down the sides of the work bowl, until smooth. Transfer to a small bowl and stir in the watercress. Season with the pepper.

2. Spread 6 bread slices with the salmon butter, leaving a ⅛-inch border around all sides, and top with the remaining bread to make 8 sandwiches. Place on a platter, cover tightly with plastic wrap, and refrigerate until the butter is chilled (this facilitates cutting the sandwiches), about 30 minutes.

3. Stack 3 sandwiches, trim off the crusts with a serrated knife, and cut diagonally twice to make 12 triangle-shaped mini-sandwiches. Keeping the sandwiches stacked, wrap each stack in plastic wrap and refrigerate until ready to serve. (The sandwiches can be prepared up to 1 day ahead, wrapped tightly, and refrigerated.)

4. Arrange the sandwiches on a serving platter and garnish with watercress sprigs. Serve immediately.

Chicken Cutlets in Wild Mushroom—Marsala Sauce

Makes 8 servings

Make Ahead: The chicken and sauce can be prepared up to 4 hours ahead. Reheat together just before serving.

Quick-cooking boneless, skinless chicken breasts are a boon to the busy cook. In fact, if you allow them to cook too long, you will end up with dry chicken, which no one enjoys. The methods employed in this dish are all about keeping the chicken nice and juicy. The chicken breasts can be served whole, but sliced they are easier to eat. You will need a deep 12-inch skillet, or divide the chicken and sauce between two smaller skillets.

8 boneless, skinless chicken breasts, lightly pounded to an even thickness

1 teaspoon salt, plus more to taste

½ teaspoon freshly ground black pepper, plus more to taste

2 tablespoons vegetable oil, as needed

1¼ cups dry Marsala

4 tablespoons (½ stick) unsalted butter, divided

2 medium onions, finely chopped

20 ounces assorted "wild" mushrooms, such as cremini and stemmed shiitake caps, thinly sliced

1 tablespoon porcini powder (see Note), optional

⅓ cup all-purpose flour

One 14½-ounce can reduced-sodium chicken broth

½ cup heavy cream

Chopped fresh parsley, to taste

1. Season the chicken with the salt and pepper. Heat the vegetable oil in a deep 12-inch skillet over high heat. In batches without crowding, add the chicken to the skillet and cook until the undersides are lightly browned, about 2 minutes. Turn and brown the other side, about 2 more minutes. (The idea is to brown the chicken, not cook it through.) Transfer to the baking dish. (The chicken can be prepared up to 4 hours ahead, cooled, covered with aluminum foil, and refrigerated.)

2. Pour the Marsala into the skillet and bring to a boil, scraping up all the browned bits in the pan with a wooden spatula. Pour the Marsala into a bowl and set aside.

3. Add 1 tablespoon of the butter to the skillet and melt. Add the onions and cook, stirring often, until golden brown, about 5 minutes. Transfer the onions to a bowl and set aside. Melt the remaining 3 tablespoons butter in the skillet. Add the mushrooms and cook, stirring often, until their juices evaporate and they start to brown, about 10 minutes. Stir in the reserved onions and the porcini powder, if using. Sprinkle with the flour and mix well. Stir in the reserved Marsala, the broth, and the cream. Bring to a boil over high heat. Season the sauce with salt and pepper. (The sauce can be prepared up to 4 hours ahead, cooled, covered, and refrigerated. Reheat in the skillet over medium heat until simmering.)

4. Return the chicken to the skillet. Simmer until the chicken shows no sign of pink when pierced in the center with the tip of a sharp knife, about 10 minutes.

5. Transfer the chicken to a platter. (If desired, let the chicken stand for 5 minutes. Holding the knife at an angle, cut the chicken across the grain into thick, wide slices. Transfer the sliced chicken to the platter.) Pour the sauce over the chicken and sprinkle with parsley. Serve hot.

Note: Porcini powder, which is simply ground dried porcini mushrooms, can be found at specialty grocers. But it is easy to make at home. Just process dried porcini mushrooms in a mini–food processor or blender into a powder. Stored in an airtight container at room temperature, the powder will keep for up to a year.

Bow-Tie Pasta with Snow Peas and Dill

Makes 8 to 10 servings

Make Ahead: The snow peas can be prepared up to 6 hours ahead, and stored at room temperature. Cook the pasta and toss with the remaining ingredients just before serving.

This pasta side dish is good enough to serve as a main course. You have the choice of moistening the pasta with heavy cream or extra virgin olive oil—they are both excellent. It can be served immediately after making, or even cooled to room temperature.

12 ounces snow peas, trimmed

1 pound bow-tie (farfalle) pasta

2 tablespoons unsalted butter

6 scallions, white and green parts, chopped

½ cup heavy cream or ⅓ cup extra virgin olive oil

½ cup (2 ounces) freshly grated Parmesan cheese

¼ cup chopped fresh dill

Salt and freshly ground black pepper, to taste

1. Bring a large pot of lightly salted water to a boil over high heat. Add the snow peas and cook just until the color changes to bright green, about 1 minute. Using a skimmer or a wire sieve, scoop the peas out of the water and transfer to a colander. Rinse under cold water and drain. Pat dry with paper towels. (The snow peas can be prepared up to 6 hours ahead and kept at room temperature.)

2. Add the pasta to the water and cook until barely tender, about 8 minutes. During the last 30 seconds, return the snow peas to the water so they can heat through. Drain the pasta and peas well.

3. While the pasta drains, melt the butter in the pasta pot over medium heat. Add the scallions and cook until wilted, about 2 minutes. Add the cream and bring to a simmer (if using olive oil, cook just until warm).

4. Return the pasta and peas to the pot and cook, stirring occasionally, until piping hot, about 1 minute. Stir in the cheese and dill. Season with the salt and pepper. Transfer to a serving dish and serve immediately or cool to room temperature.

Glazed Baby Carrots with Currants

Makes 8 servings
Make Ahead: The carrots can be prepared 1 day ahead.

Carrots are a great unifier in menus. They go with so many dishes, and always add bright color to the plate. Here, currants harmonize with the sweet carrots.

1½ pounds baby-cut carrots

2 tablespoons unsalted butter

2 tablespoons light brown sugar

⅓ cup dried currants

Salt and freshly ground black pepper, to taste

1. Bring a large pot of lightly salted water to a boil over high heat. Add the baby carrots and cook until barely tender, about 5 minutes. Drain and rinse under cold water. Drain well.

2. Melt the butter in a large skillet over medium heat. Add the carrots, brown sugar, and ¼ cup water. Cook, stirring often, until the carrots are heated through and the liquid has evaporated into a glaze, about 5 minutes. Stir in the currants. Season with salt and pepper. (The carrots can be prepared up to 1 day ahead. Reheat in a covered skillet with 2 tablespoons water.) Transfer to a serving dish and serve hot.

Strawberry-Almond Ice Cream Cake

Makes 8 to 12 servings
Make Ahead: The cake can be made 1 day ahead. The sauce can be made 1 day ahead.

Ice cream cakes have many virtues, not the least of which is their easy preparation. This one is pretty in pink and beige, and features the harmonious combination of strawberries and almonds. If toasted almond ice cream proves difficult to find, slightly soften 2 pints vanilla ice cream and mix in 1 teaspoon almond extract and ¹/₂ cup sliced almonds, toasted and cooled.

Crust

¹⁄₃ cup sliced almonds

2 tablespoons granulated sugar

²⁄₃ cup crushed vanilla wafer crumbs (about 20 cookies)

2 tablespoons unsalted butter, melted

Filling

2 pints toasted almond ice cream, slightly softened

2 pints strawberry ice cream, slightly softened

1 cup strawberry preserves

Sauce

1 quart strawberries, hulled and sliced

¹⁄₃ cup sugar

1 tablespoon fresh lemon juice

¹⁄₂ cup heavy cream

1 tablespoon confectioners' sugar

¹⁄₂ teaspoon vanilla extract

¹⁄₄ cup sliced almonds, toasted (see Note)

1. Position a rack in the center of the oven and preheat to 350°F. Lightly oil a 9-inch springform pan.

2. To make the crust, process the almonds and sugar in a food processor until the almonds are ground into a powder. Add the crumbs and pulse to combine. Add the butter and process until the mixture is evenly moistened. Press evenly into the springform pan.

3. Bake until the crust looks set and the crumbs are very lightly toasted, about 10 minutes. Cool completely.

4. Soften the toasted almond ice cream at room temperature, and spread evenly in the cooled shell. Your fingers work as well as anything; if they get too

cold, cover the ice cream with a double thickness of plastic wrap to act as a barrier. Spread with the strawberry preserves. Freeze the cake, uncovered, until the ice cream is firm, about 15 minutes.

5. Soften the strawberry ice cream at room temperature, and spread evenly over the almond ice cream. Cover with plastic wrap and freeze at least 4 hours. (The cake can be made up to 1 day ahead.)

6. To make the sauce, process the strawberries, sugar, and lemon juice in a food processor until smooth. (The sauce can be made up to 1 day ahead, covered, and refrigerated.)

7. When ready to serve, run a hot, wet knife around the inside edge of the cake pan and remove the sides. Transfer the cake on the pan bottom to a serving plate. Whip the cream, confectioners' sugar, and vanilla in a chilled medium bowl with an electric mixer until stiff. If you have a pastry bag, fit it with a ½-inch open star tip, fill it with the whipped cream, and pipe rosettes around the edge of the cake; sprinkle with the almonds. Lacking a bag, spread the whipped cream over the top of the cake with an icing spatula and sprinkle with the nuts. Using a sharp knife dipped into a glass of hot water, cut the pie into wedges and serve with the strawberry sauce.

Note: To toast almonds, spread the nuts on a baking sheet. Bake in a preheated 350°F oven, stirring occasionally, until the almonds are toasted, about 12 minutes. Cool completely.

Jackie O's

Makes about 6 cocktails
Make Ahead: Make the cocktails just before serving.

During a barhopping trek not long ago with my friend Carrie Phillips, who is the picture of a hip young working girl, she ordered a Jackie O, a new cocktail on the scene. After sneaking a sip, I knew it would be the perfect drink for this shower menu—feminine and classy. Jackie O's are usually shaken and served up, but for a party, it is more convenient to make them by the pitcherful. If you have a bunch of martini glasses and want to serve the drinks in the classic style, add a generous amount of ice cubes to the pitcher and let the beverage chill well before pouring. But no one will turn down one on the rocks.

2 cups unsweetened pineapple juice

1 cup vodka

¼ cup apricot brandy

1 tablespoon grenadine

Pour the pineapple juice, vodka, apricot brandy, and grenadine in a pitcher, and stir well. Pour into 6 tall ice-filled glasses and serve.

A Spring Shower Shopping List

Serves 8

Dairy

Unsalted butter (2¼ sticks)

Heavy cream (1 cup plus ½ cup, if using for
pasta)

Parmesan cheese (2 ounces)

Delicatessen

Smoked salmon, sliced (4 ounces)

Frozen

2 pints strawberry ice cream

2 pints toasted almond or vanilla ice cream

Groceries

Almond extract (1 teaspoon, if needed to make
toasted almond ice cream)

Sliced almonds (about ½ cup, plus ½ cup
more, if toasted almond ice cream is
unavailable)

Chicken broth, reduced-sodium (one
14½-ounce can)

Dried currants (⅓ cup)

Farfalle pasta (1 pound)

Pineapple juice, unsweetened (2 cups)

Porcini mushroom powder (1 tablespoon,
optional)

Strawberry preserves (1 cup)

Thin-sliced white sandwich bread (16 slices)

Vanilla wafer cookies (⅔ cup crushed crumbs)

Liquor

Apricot brandy (¼ cup)

Grenadine (1 tablespoon)

Dry Marsala (1¼ cups)

Vodka (1 cup)

Meat

Chicken breasts, boneless and skinless (8)

Pantry Staples

Extra virgin olive oil (⅓ cup, if using for pasta)

Vegetable oil (2 tablespoons)

All-purpose flour (⅓ cup)

Confectioners' sugar (1 tablespoon)

Granulated sugar (about ½ cup)

Light brown sugar (2 tablespoons)

Produce

Baby-cut carrots (1½ pounds)

Dill (1 bunch)

"Wild" mushrooms, such as cremini
(20 ounces)

Yellow onions (2 medium)

Scallions (1 bunch)

Snow peas (12 ounces)

Strawberries (1 quart)

Watercress (1 bunch)

A Spring Shower Preparation Timetable

1 day ahead

Make sandwiches; refrigerate

Make carrots; refrigerate

Make ice cream cake; freeze

6 hours before serving

Blanch snow peas; store at room temperature

4 hours before serving

Make chicken and sauce; refrigerate

2 hours before serving

Make pasta, if serving at room temperature

Just before serving

Make cocktails

Make pasta, if serving hot

Reheat chicken in sauce

Reheat carrots

A Mother's Day Brunch

Like many families, ours always took Mom out for brunch on Mother's Day. Under the best of circumstances, brunch is a lovely meal. Without the usual time constraints of weekday meals, it is a chance to linger over a second (or third) cup of coffee and enjoy longer conver-

---

Serves 6

Baked Mascarpone-Stuffed French Toast

Berry-Maple Compote

Pork Breakfast Loaf with Fresh Herbs

Mimosa Sunrise

---

sations with friends and family. However, it was the rare restaurant that didn't keep us waiting for our reserved table on this popular "holiday," and eventually, brunch out became brunch in.

Because a Mother's Day brunch should be indulgent, this menu is purposely rich and decadent. French toast is a Sunday morning favorite. For years, I've been making sandwiches with the sliced bread to add interest to this classic, using preserves, chocolate, or other sweets as a filling, and this time I've used creamy mascarpone. To avoid a snafu on the griddle, bake the

French toast in an ovenproof serving dish. Maple syrup–laced berry compote serves as the sauce. For a meaty brunch side dish, the herbed pork meat loaf can't be beat, and it is much easier than frying bacon or sausage in a skillet. Because this meal is pleasantly over the top, I don't offer an appetizer, as it could tax most people's appetites. If you wish, you could put out smoked salmon and thinly sliced bagels, but warn the guests not to fill up on the nibbles.

And what's a brunch without champagne or, more to the point, Mimosas? A splash of grenadine gives the cocktails a festive look. With a menu this extravagant, there's really no need for dessert, so just raise another Mimosa Sunrise to Mom.

Baked Mascarpone-Stuffed French Toast

Makes 6 servings

Make Ahead: The sandwiches can be prepared the night before, covered, and refrigerated, then dipped in the egg mixture the next morning before baking.

French toast is one of the first things I learned how to cook, thanks to my parents, who were sure their sons knew how to get around in the kitchen. For a small group, it's no problem to sauté up a stack or two, but for large groups, try this baked method. You want unsliced golden, egg-enriched bread for this dish—challah is preferred, but other choices include brioche loaf, Hawaiian, Portuguese sweet, or Texan bread. Spoon the Berry-Maple Compote (page 111) over the top or use plain maple syrup.

1 unsliced loaf (about 1 pound) egg-enriched bread (see suggestions above), preferably slightly stale

8 ounces mascarpone, at room temperature

6 large eggs

3 cups milk

⅓ cup sugar

2 teaspoons vanilla extract

2 tablespoons unsalted butter, melted

Berry-Maple Compote (page 111) or pure maple syrup, for serving

1. Using a serrated knife held at a slight angle to make larger slices, cut the bread into twelve ¾-inch thick slices. Spread equal amounts of the mascarpone on 6 slices, then top with the remaining slices to make sandwiches. (The sandwiches can be prepared the night before baking, covered loosely with plastic wrap, and refrigerated.)

2. Position a rack in the center of the oven and preheat to 350°F. Lightly butter a 15 × 10-inch baking dish.

3. Arrange the sandwiches snugly in the dish. Whisk the eggs, milk, sugar, and vanilla in a large bowl to combine. Pour the custard over the sandwiches. Let

stand 5 minutes. Spoon the pooled custard around the sandwiches over the tops to allow the sandwiches to soak up as much custard as possible.

4. Bake for 30 minutes. Drizzle the melted butter over the top and continue baking until puffed and golden, about 15 minutes.

5. Let stand for 5 minutes. Serve hot, allowing 1 sandwich per serving, with the compote or syrup.

Berry-Maple Compote

Makes 6 to 8 servings
Make Ahead: The compote can be prepared up to 1 day ahead.

This compote is made deliberately syrupy so it can work as a topping for the Baked Mascarpone-Stuffed French Toast (page 109). If you are making the compote in the winter, you may want to substitute frozen blueberries and raspberries for expensive imported fresh ones.

1 cup (½ pint) fresh or frozen blueberries

1 cup (½ pint) fresh or frozen raspberries

¾ cup pure maple syrup

1 quart fresh strawberries, hulled and sliced

1. Bring the blueberries, raspberries, and maple syrup to a simmer over medium heat. Cook until the berries soften and give off juices, about 5 minutes. Remove from the heat and cool. (The compote can be prepared up to this point 1 day ahead, covered, and refrigerated. Bring to room temperature before serving.)

2. Stir in the strawberries. Serve at room temperature.

Pork Breakfast Loaf with Fresh Herbs

Makes 8 servings

Make Ahead: The meat loaf can be made up to 1 day ahead.

This hearty meat loaf is just the thing to accompany French toast, waffles, pancakes, or any other griddled breakfast fare. It has the flavor of link sausage, but its baked loaf shape makes it easier to serve. Leftovers make very good sandwiches.

2 large eggs

½ cup dried bread crumbs

¼ cup finely chopped shallots

2 tablespoons finely chopped fresh sage

2 tablespoons finely chopped fresh parsley

1½ teaspoons salt

½ teaspoon freshly ground black pepper

2 pounds ground pork

1. Position a rack in the center of the oven and preheat to 350°F. Lightly oil an 8½ × 4½-inch loaf pan.

2. Mix the eggs, bread crumbs, shallots, sage, parsley, salt, and pepper in a large bowl. Add the pork and mix well with clean hands until combined. Pack into the loaf pan. Place the pan on a rimmed baking sheet.

3. Bake until an instant-read thermometer inserted in the center of the loaf reads 165°F, 1 to 1¼ hours. Let stand for 5 minutes. (The meat loaf can be made up to 1 day ahead, cooled, wrapped in aluminum foil, and refrigerated. Reheat, wrapped in foil, in a 350°F oven until heated through, about 30 minutes. Or reheat in a microwave oven on Medium power, the meat loaf loosely wrapped in microwave-safe plastic wrap, for about 8 minutes.)

4. Slice the meat loaf and serve hot.

Mimosa Sunrise

Makes 1 drink

One of the most attractive cocktails you'll ever lay eyes on, this combines elements of a Mimosa and a Tequila Sunrise. Use a high-quality California or French sparkling wine, and save the vintage Champagne for another time. Because champagne glasses (use flutes, not coupes, for the best appearance) have different volumes, the measurements in the recipe are estimates for one drink in a standard flute—allow one-third orange juice, two-thirds sparkling wine, and a good splash of grenadine. No one likes warm sparkling wine, so be sure to use well-chilled ingredients; chilling the flutes in the freezer will help, too. You will get about 8 servings from a 750-ml bottle of sparkling wine.

3 tablespoons chilled fresh orange juice

6 tablespoons chilled good-quality sparkling wine

1 teaspoon chilled grenadine

Place a long spoon, such as an iced tea or bar spoon, in a chilled champagne flute. (This keeps the sparkling wine from frothing over when it comes into contact with the orange juice, a natural reaction caused by the carbon dioxide and alcohol in the wine and the sugar in the juice.) Add the orange juice. Slowly pour in the sparkling wine, being careful that the wine doesn't froth over. Slowly dribble the grenadine down the inside of the glass. (See Note.) Serve immediately.

Note: If you are making a few drinks at once, line up the glasses and add the juice to each glass. Starting at one end, pour a splash of sparkling wine into each glass. Go back to the first glass and repeat a few times until the glasses are filled to about 1 inch from the tops. This allows frothing to disperse gradually and keeps the bartender from waiting for each serving to settle before moving on to the next. Finish with the grenadine.

A Mother's Day Brunch Shopping List

Serves 6

Dairy/Refrigerated

Unsalted butter (2 tablespoons)

Large eggs (8)

Mascarpone (8 ounces)

Milk (3 cups)

Orange juice, fresh squeezed (1 pint)

Groceries

Challah or other egg-enriched bread (one
1-pound loaf, unsliced)

Dried bread crumbs ($\frac{1}{2}$ cup)

Maple syrup ($\frac{3}{4}$ cup)

Liquor and Related Ingredients

Good-quality sparkling wine (one 750-ml bottle)

Grenadine (about 3 tablespoons)

Meat

Ground pork (2 pounds)

Pantry Staples

Granulated sugar ($\frac{1}{3}$ cup)

Vanilla extract (2 teaspoons)

Produce

Blueberries (1 pint or use frozen)

Parsley (1 bunch)

Raspberries (1 pint or use frozen)

Sage (1 bunch)

Shallots (2 medium, for $\frac{1}{4}$ cup chopped)

Strawberries (1 quart)

A Mother's Day Brunch Preparation Timetable

1 day ahead

Make the raspberry-blueberry base for the compote; refrigerate

Make meat loaf; refrigerate

The night before

Make mascarpone sandwiches for French toast; refrigerate

30 minutes before serving

Reheat meat loaf

Just before serving

Make Mimosa Sunrises

Bake French toast

Add sliced strawberries to compote

Part Three

Summer on a
Plate

A Memorial Day Barbecue Season Kickoff

The last weekend of May, which precedes Memorial Day, is the official beginning to the outdoor cooking season, and the first time of the year when many cooks fire up the grill. For some, as the gas grill rises in popularity, barbecuing has become a year-

Serves 8

Cedar-Smoked Salmon with Cucumber Salsa

Provençal Potato and Fennel Salad

Sugar Snap Peas in Tarragon Vinaigrette

Grilled Pineapple Sundaes with Caramel Rum Sauce

round pastime. I know lots of people who wear down parkas to ward off the chill as they grill the Christmas turkey in the carport. Nonetheless, cooking outdoors is a much more pleasant experience with the warmth of the sun on your back.

In the late spring and summer, even city dwellers can find themselves face-to-face with an outdoor grill. These confrontations can take place in the backyard of a rented vacation home or during a weekend visit to a beach or park. No matter where the first seasonal meeting between human and grill takes place, the irresistible flavor and aroma of grilled food set the stage for a solid three months of outdoor cooking and entertaining whenever the mood strikes—or when warm weather requires a respite from a steamy kitchen.

I used to be quite curmudgeonly about gas grills because they don't provide the same wood-kissed flavor as their charcoal counterparts. While I still prefer a charcoal grill, I now own a gas model, too. I use the convenient gas grill for weeknight meals, and build a fire in the charcoal grill on weekends when I can spare the extra twenty minutes or so to light the coals.

There is a temptation to grill everything in sight, but hold back. One or two items per menu are workable; more than that can lead to a traffic jam on your grill. In this menu, both the main course (cedar-smoked salmon with cucumber salsa) and the dessert (grilled pineapple sundaes with caramel rum sauce) are grilled, and that is enough. Round out the meal with a potato salad and sugar snap peas in vinaigrette, and you have a refreshing meal that is ideal for a leisurely dinner, as the French say, *en plein air*.

Cedar-Smoked Salmon with Cucumber Salsa

Makes 8 servings

Make Ahead: The salsa can be made up to 8 hours ahead.

Grilling fish on planks of untreated cedar is a popular cooking technique in the Northwest that has spread throughout the country. The planks are easily available at kitchenware stores. Served with a crisp cucumber salsa, this is a restaurant-style dish that can be easily re-created at home.

Cucumber Salsa

3 large cucumbers

1 teaspoon salt

1 scallion, white and green parts, finely chopped

3 tablespoons chopped cilantro, basil, or parsley

3 tablespoons fresh lemon juice

1 jalapeño, seeded and minced

¼ cup extra virgin olive oil

2 tablespoons fresh lemon juice

One 3½-pound salmon fillet, thin belly strip trimmed (see Note)

1 untreated cedar plank for grilling, soaked in water for 1 hour and drained

½ teaspoon salt

½ teaspoon freshly ground black pepper

1. To make the salsa, peel each cucumber and cut in half lengthwise. Using a dessert spoon, scoop out the seeds. Cut the cucumbers into ½-inch cubes and place in a colander. Toss with the salt. Let stand to drain for 30 minutes. Rinse the cucumbers well, drain, and pat dry with paper towels.

2. Mix the cucumbers with the scallion, cilantro, lemon juice, and jalapeño. Cover and refrigerate until chilled, at least 1 hour. (The salsa can be made up to 8 hours ahead.)

3. Whisk the oil and lemon juice in a glass or ceramic dish just large enough to hold the salmon. Add the salmon and turn to coat. Let stand at room temperature for 30 minutes, no longer.

4. Meanwhile, build a charcoal fire (use about 4 pounds briquettes) on one side of an outdoor grill and let burn until the coals are covered with white ash. For a gas grill, turn one burner on High and leave the other burner(s) off.

5. Place the drained cedar plank over the coals (or hot side of the grill). Heat, turning occasionally, until the plank is hot, about 4 minutes. Remove the salmon from the marinade, season with the salt and pepper, and place on the hot plank. Place the plank over the cooler (unlighted) side of the grill and cover. Grill until the salmon has turned opaque with a rosy center when flaked with the tip of a sharp knife, about 20 minutes. Using two large spatulas or a rimless baking sheet, transfer the salmon to a long serving platter.

6. Cut the salmon lengthwise in half, then crosswise into portions, and serve with the cucumber salsa passed on the side.

Note: A whole, untrimmed salmon fillet includes a narrow strip of salmon flesh that runs the entire length of the fillet. Located at the belly of the fish, and much thinner than the rest of the fillet, this tasty section will overcook unless it is removed. Often, the fishmonger will only sell the entire untrimmed fillet, expecting the cook to trim off the unwanted portion (kind of like a butcher who sells a roast with a bit too much surface fat). In order to get the 3½-pound trimmed salmon fillet for this recipe, you may have to purchase a 4¼-pound untrimmed fillet. Simply cut it off in one long strip where the rest of the fillet begins to thicken noticeably. Save it for another use, such as salmon kebabs or salad, or grill it right next to the larger fillet, allowing about 10 minutes total cooking time.

Provençal Potato and Fennel Salad

Makes 8 servings
Make Ahead: The salad can be made 1 day ahead.

Potato salad is one of those side dishes that seem to go with so many foods. I love coming up with new potato salad recipes to match with specific entrées. I created this one to go with grilled fish, which it does very nicely.

¼ cup white or red wine vinegar

3 tablespoons finely chopped shallots

2 teaspoons Dijon mustard

1 garlic clove, crushed through a press

½ teaspoon salt, plus more to taste

½ teaspoon freshly ground black pepper, plus more to taste

1 cup extra virgin olive oil

3 pounds red-skinned potatoes, scrubbed

One medium bulb fennel, fronds trimmed, cut into ½-inch dice (2 cups)

½ cup pitted and chopped black Mediterranean olives

One 12-ounce jar roasted red peppers, drained, rinsed, and chopped (¾ cup)

3 tablespoons chopped fresh parsley

1. Whisk the vinegar, shallots, mustard, garlic, salt, and pepper in a medium bowl. Gradually whisk in the oil to make a thick vinaigrette. Set aside.

2. Place the potatoes in a large pot of lightly salted water and bring to a boil over high heat. Reduce the heat to medium-low and cook until the potatoes are tender when pierced with the tip of a knife, about 25 minutes. Drain and rinse under cold running water until the potatoes are easy to handle.

3. Slice the warm potatoes into a large bowl. Add the fennel, olives, and red peppers, and mix well. Toss with half of the vinaigrette. Separately cover and refrigerate the potato salad and vinaigrette until the salad is chilled, at least 2 hours. (The salad can be made 1 day ahead.)

4. When ready to serve, toss the salad with the remaining vinaigrette and the parsley. Season with salt and pepper. Serve chilled.

Sugar Snap Peas in Tarragon Vinaigrette

Makes 8 servings

Make Ahead: The sugar snap peas can be prepared 1 day ahead. Make the salad just before serving.

Although you can generally get them year-round at the produce market, the local sugar snap peas that appear in late spring farmers' markets are unsurpassed for sweetness. They make an exceptional salad. Dress them with the vinaigrette just before serving—if allowed to stand, their bright green will turn drab.

2 pounds sugar snap peas, trimmed

1½ tablespoons sherry vinegar

½ teaspoon sugar

¼ teaspoon salt, plus more to taste

⅛ teaspoon freshly ground black pepper, plus more to taste

⅓ cup plus 1 tablespoon extra virgin olive oil

2 scallions, white and green parts, chopped

2 tablespoons chopped fresh tarragon

1. Bring a large pot of lightly salted water to a boil over high heat. Add the sugar snap peas and cook just until the peas are crisp-tender, about 3 minutes (the water may not come back to a boil). Drain and transfer to a large bowl of ice water to stop the cooking. Drain again and pat the peas dry with paper towels. (The sugar snap peas can be prepared up to 1 day ahead, wrapped in paper towels, and refrigerated in plastic bags.)

2. Whisk the vinegar, sugar, salt, and pepper in a medium bowl. Gradually whisk in the oil.

3. Just before serving mix the sugar snap peas, the vinaigrette, scallions, and tarragon in a medium bowl. Season with salt and pepper. Serve immediately.

Grilled Pineapple Sundaes with Caramel Rum Sauce

Makes 8 servings

Make Ahead: The sauce can be made up to 3 days ahead.

Any warm dessert with ice cream automatically gets extra points with my guests. The interplay between hot and cold, tangy and sweet makes this treat extra-special. I give two sets of game plans, one for a gas grill and the other for a charcoal grill for grilling the pineapple after smoking the salmon.

Caramel Rum Sauce

1 cup sugar

2 cups heavy cream, heated

2 tablespoons golden or dark rum

½ teaspoon vanilla extract

1 ripe pineapple, pared, cored, and cut crosswise into
   8 slices

1 quart vanilla ice cream

1. To make the sauce, pour ¼ cup water in a heavy-bottomed medium saucepan. Add the sugar and cook over high heat, stirring just until the sugar melts. Cook without stirring, occasionally swirling the saucepan by the handle and brushing down any crystals that form on the side of the pan with a wet natural-bristle pastry brush, until the sugar has caramelized to a dark copper-brown (think of the color of a new penny), 3 to 5 minutes.

2. Slowly pour in the hot cream—the mixture will bubble up, so be very careful. Boil, stirring often, until the sauce has reduced to 2 cups, about 3 minutes. Remove from the heat and stir in the rum and vanilla. Cool to room temperature. (The sauce can be made up to 3 days ahead, cooled, covered, and refrigerated. Reheat in the top part of a double boiler over boiling water.)

3. To grill the pineapple after cooking an entrée in a charcoal grill, toss about 20 more briquets on the fire and let them burn down while you serve the entrée. For a gas grill, turn the heat down to Medium.

If you are cooking the pineapple without previously grilling an entrée, build a charcoal fire in an outdoor grill and let burn until the coals are covered with white ash and medium hot (you should be able to hold your hand over the grill grate for about 3 seconds). In a gas grill, heat the grill on High, then reduce the heat to Medium.

4. If you have cooked food on the grill, scrub it well with a grill brush to remove any residual drippings. Lightly oil the grill. Place the pineapple on the grill. Grill the pineapple until the undersides have grill marks, about 3 minutes. Turn the pineapple and cook until the other sides are marked, about 3 minutes. Transfer the pineapple to a cutting board, and coarsely chop into bite-sized pieces. Let cool for 5 to 10 minutes.

5. Scoop the ice cream into 8 bowls. Top with the warm pineapple and its juices, then with the caramel sauce. Serve immediately.

A Memorial Day Barbecue Season Kickoff Shopping List

Serves 8

Dairy

Heavy cream (1 pint)

Fish

Salmon fillet (one 3½-pound fillet)

Frozen

Vanilla ice cream (1 quart)

Groceries

Black Mediterranean olives (½ cup pitted and
     chopped)

Roasted red peppers (one 12-ounce jar)

Liquor

Golden or dark rum (2 tablespoons)

Miscellaneous

Cedar plank for grilling (1, available at kitchen-
     ware shops)

Pantry Staples

Dijon mustard (2 teaspoons)

Extra virgin olive oil (about 2 cups)

Sherry vinegar (1½ tablespoons)

White or red wine vinegar (¼ cup)

Sugar (1 cup)

Vanilla extract (½ teaspoon)

Produce

Cilantro (1 bunch)

Cucumbers (3 large)

Fennel (1 medium bulb)

Garlic (1 head)

Jalapeño (1)

Lemons (2 medium, for 5 tablespoons fresh
     lemon juice)

Parsley (1 bunch)

Pineapple (1 ripe)

Red-skinned potatoes (3 pounds)

Scallions (3)

Shallots (1 large, for 3 tablespoons chopped)

Sugar snap peas (2 pounds)

A Memorial Day Barbecue Season Kickoff Preparation Timetable

3 days ahead

Make caramel sauce; refrigerate

1 day ahead

Make potato salad; refrigerate

Blanch sugar snap peas; refrigerate

8 hours ahead

Make salsa; refrigerate

30 minutes before grilling salmon

Marinate salmon

Build charcoal fire or preheat gas grill

Just before serving

Grill salmon

Add remaining vinaigrette to potato salad; reseason

Finish sugar snap pea salad

Just before serving dessert

Grill pineapple

Reheat caramel sauce

A Father's Day Cookout

Father's Day is the perfect time for a cookout. The weather is usually warm without being aggressively hot. Summer produce is beginning to appear, and the garden is finally taking off and showing some blooms.

People used to think of grilling as a man's job. Although

Serves 8

Chicken Fajita Nachos

Hickory-Smoked Baby Back Ribs with Vidalia Onion BBQ Sauce

Hearty Barbecued Beans

Caesar Coleslaw

Mango-Macadamia Crisp

---

that's all changed (I have equal numbers of men and women in my grilling classes), many of us have memories of Dad outside at the grill. For men of my generation (and this is probably still true of today's young cooks, be they boys or girls), it was a tradition to learn how to grill from your dad. So, in spite of how many women are grilling these days, it is appropriate that this Father's Day menu has a grilled entrée.

Speaking of grilling, more households have gas grills than

charcoal grills, so I give instructions on how to use either grill. I am a charcoal-grill fan. Gas grills get the job done, but lack that extra layer of smoky flavor. If you have the room in your back-yard, I advise both grills. When you have the time to set up the charcoal grill, do so. On weeknights when you want to toss something on the grill quickly without the fuss of building a fire, use the gas grill.

The tone of the menu is very relaxed, and every item on the menu can be made in advance. To be sure that Dad gets extra time in the hammock, there is very little last-minute attention required. Even the ribs are prepared in a special method that ensures tender results without fire flare-ups that plague other techniques. Dad's supposed to have the day off—you don't want him having to hang around the grill, helping you put out fires!

Chicken Fajita Nachos

Makes 8 servings

Make Ahead: The chicken can be prepared up to 8 hours ahead. The vegetables can be prepared up to 2 hours ahead. Assemble the nachos just before baking.

The only problem with nachos as an appetizer is trying not to eat too many before dinner. This version, with lots of chicken and vegetables, could almost be a main course, so restraint is required! Since the baking dish will double as the serving platter, use something attractive. Look for glazed terra-cotta nacho servers, about 12 inches wide and 2 inches deep, or use any large, round ovenproof metal platter or even a pizza pan.

2 tablespoons lime juice

2 tablespoons extra virgin olive oil, divided

½ teaspoon salt

¼ teaspoon freshly ground black pepper

Vegetable oil cooking spray

Two 7-ounce boneless and skinless chicken breasts, lightly pounded to an even thickness

1 medium onion, chopped

1 small red bell pepper, seeded and chopped into ½-inch dice

1 jalapeño, seeded and finely chopped

2 garlic cloves, chopped

6 ounces (½ of a 12-ounce bag) tortilla chips

1½ cups (6 ounces) shredded sharp Cheddar cheese

1. To prepare the chicken, place the lime juice, 1 tablespoon oil, salt, and pepper in a zippered plastic bag, close, and shake the bag to combine. Add the chicken breasts, close, and refrigerate for at least 1 hour and up to 4 hours, turning the bag occasionally.

2. Spray a large nonstick skillet with vegetable oil. Heat the skillet over medium-high heat. Remove the chicken breasts from the marinade and place in the skillet. Cook until the underside is nicely browned, about 3 minutes. Turn and brown the other side, about 3 minutes more. Reduce the heat to medium and cook until the chicken springs back when pressed in the center, about 6 minutes. Remove from the heat and cool. Chop the chicken into ¾-inch bite-sized

pieces. (The chicken can be prepared up to 8 hours ahead, cooled, covered, and refrigerated.)

3. Heat the remaining 1 tablespoon oil in a medium saucepan over medium heat. Add the onion, red bell pepper, jalapeño, and garlic, and cover. Cook, stirring often, until the onion is tender, about 6 minutes. (The vegetables can be prepared up to 2 hours ahead and kept at room temperature.)

4. Position a rack in the upper third of the oven and preheat to 450°F.

5. Spread the tortilla chips on a 12- to 14-inch nacho server, ovenproof platter, or pizza pan. Top with the chicken, then the vegetables. Sprinkle with the cheese. Bake until the cheese melts, about 5 minutes.

Hickory-Smoked Baby Back Ribs with Vidalia Onion BBQ Sauce

Makes 8 servings

Make Ahead: The spice-rubbed ribs can be refrigerated 1 day ahead. The cooked ribs can be made up to 4 hours ahead, and glazed just before serving.

There are many ways to grill ribs, but whenever I teach this method in my cooking classes, I gain a whole new group of converts. The trick is to wrap the ribs in aluminum foil, then bake the ribs in the foil so they have a chance to cook in their own juices. (The ribs can even be prepared a few hours ahead at this point.) The ribs are then unwrapped and grilled with lots of hickory smoke, and brushed with a sweet-tangy sauce to give them a glaze. I think you'll like the results.

¼ cup chili powder

1 tablespoon salt

7 pounds baby back ribs, cut into slabs

2 cup hickory chips, soaked in water for at least 30 minutes

Vidalia Onion BBQ Sauce (page 134)

1. Mix the chili powder and salt in a small bowl. Sprinkle the ribs with the spice mixture. Wrap each slab of ribs in aluminum foil. Let the ribs stand at room temperature for 1 hour. (The wrapped ribs can be refrigerated up to 1 day ahead; remove from the refrigerator 1 hour before baking.)

2. Position racks in the center and top third of the oven and preheat to 350°F.

3. Place the foil-wrapped ribs on baking sheets (they can overlap). Bake until the ribs are just tender (open a foil packet to check), about 1½ hours. (The ribs can be prepared up to 1 day ahead, cooled, and refrigerated.)

4. Meanwhile, build a charcoal fire in an outdoor grill and let burn until the coals are covered with white ash. Sprinkle the drained chips over the grill—they will begin to smoke almost immediately. For a gas grill, place the drained chips on a piece of aluminum foil. Place the foil directly on the source of heat. Preheat the grill on High, allowing about 30 minutes for the chips to smolder and give off

smoke (be patient, as some grills take longer than others). Reduce the heat to Medium.

5. Unwrap the ribs, discarding the juices and rendered fat, and place on the grill. Cover and grill until the ribs are browned, about 5 minutes. Turn, cover, and brown the other side, about 5 minutes more. Brush the top of the ribs with some of the sauce and turn. Grill, covered, until the underside is glazed, about 3 minutes. Brush again with sauce, turn, cover, and grill to glaze the other side, about 3 minutes. Transfer the ribs to a cutting board and let stand for a few minutes.

6. Cut the slabs into individual ribs and transfer to a serving platter. Serve hot, with the remaining sauce passed on the side.

Note: Master grillers argue over the benefits of hardwood charcoal versus charcoal briquettes (gas grill fans are left out of this discussion). Hardwood charcoal does have superior flavor, but it burns very quickly and very hot and you have ashes before you know what happened.

Vidalia Onion BBQ Sauce

Makes about 6 cups
Make Ahead: The sauce can be made up to 2 weeks ahead.

Some kind of sweet onion (such as Maui, Walla Walla, or Texas Sweets) is available at any time of the year, but late spring is the time for Georgia's Vidalia onions. While their inherent sweetness is a fine accent to smoky ribs, keep this sauce in mind for chicken, too. If you have leftover sauce after cooking the ribs, serve it on the side as a dip, or refrigerate it for another meal. It keeps very well.

2 tablespoons unsalted butter

3 medium sweet onions, such as Vidalia, finely chopped

6 garlic cloves, finely chopped

Two 10-ounce jars sugarless peach fruit spread made
    with fruit juice

Two 12-ounce bottles American-style chili sauce

⅔ cup spicy brown mustard

½ cup light (unsulfured) molasses

⅔ cup cider vinegar

3 tablespoons Worcestershire sauce

Melt the butter in a heavy-bottomed, medium saucepan over medium-low heat. Add the onions and cover. Cook, stirring often, until the onions are golden brown, about 15 minutes. Add the garlic and cook, uncovered, until it gives off its fragrance, about 2 minutes. Stir in the peach fruit spread, chili sauce, mustard, molasses, vinegar, and Worcestershire sauce. Bring to a simmer, stirring often. Reduce the heat to low and simmer, stirring often to avoid scorching, until lightly thickened, about 30 minutes. (The sauce can be prepared up to 2 weeks ahead, cooled, covered, and refrigerated.)

Hearty Barbecued Beans

Makes 8 to 10 servings

Make Ahead: The beans can be prepared up to 1 day ahead.

Baked beans are one of the best friends ribs ever had. If you wish, add another bean variety or two to the pintos. Red, white, kidney, and garbanzo beans are all good, but don't use black beans, which will color the entire dish. And if you don't want to use bourbon, diluted apple juice is fine.

6 slices bacon

1 sweet medium onion, preferably Vidalia, chopped

1 jalapeño, seeded and minced

Four 15- to 19-ounce cans pinto beans, drained and
  rinsed

1½ cups Vidalia Onion BBQ Sauce (opposite page)

½ cup bourbon or ⅓ cup apple juice and 3 tablespoons
  water

1. Position a rack in the center of the oven and preheat to 350°F.
2. Place the bacon in a cold Dutch oven or flameproof casserole. Cook over medium-high heat, turning occasionally, until crisp, about 6 minutes. Transfer to paper towels to drain and cool, leaving the fat in the pot. Crumble the bacon.
3. Add the onion and jalapeño, and cook over medium heat, stirring occasionally, until the onions are golden, about 5 minutes. Stir in the beans and the barbecue sauce, then the bourbon and crumbled bacon. (The beans can be made up to this point 2 hours ahead, and kept at room temperature. Or cool, cover, and refrigerate for up to 1 day. Bring to a boil before proceeding.) Bring to a boil.
4. Cover and bake for 30 minutes. Uncover, stir, and continue baking until the cooking liquid has thickened, about 15 minutes. Serve hot.

Caesar Coleslaw

Makes 8 servings

Make Ahead: The slaw can be made up to 1 day ahead. Add the Parmesan cheese just before serving.

Anchovies used to be very unpopular little fishes. Now, thanks to Caesar salad and rustic cooking, the little guys are making a comeback. This bold coleslaw goes well with many grilled foods. To shred the cabbage, use the slicing blade (not the shredding blade) of a food processor or a V-slicer.

1¼ cups mayonnaise

⅓ cup lemon juice

2 teaspoons anchovy paste

2 garlic cloves, crushed through a press

1 medium head Savoy or green cabbage (2¼ pounds), cored and thinly shredded

6 scallions, white and green parts, thinly sliced

½ cup freshly grated Parmesan cheese

Salt and freshly ground black pepper, to taste

1. In a large bowl, whisk the mayonnaise, lemon juice, anchovy paste, and garlic until smooth. Add the cabbage and scallions and mix well. Cover tightly and refrigerate until chilled, at least 1 hour. (Coleslaw can be prepared up to 1 day ahead, covered, and refrigerated.)

2. Just before serving, mix in the cheese. Season with the salt and pepper. Serve chilled.

Mango-Macadamia Crisp

Makes 8 servings

Make Ahead: The mangoes can be sliced up to 8 hours ahead, covered, and refrigerated. The topping can be prepared up to 8 hours ahead. The crisp can be made 4 hours ahead, but it is best served right from the oven.

Mangoes, which taste like peaches on a tropical vacation, are a great summer fruit for baking into cobblers, pies, and crisps. Macadamia nuts are an extravagant addition to the topping for this crisp, but it's Dad's day and he deserves something special. Unsalted macadamia nuts work best. If you can't find them, rinse the salted nuts in a wire sieve, and then pat dry before chopping. Don't chop the macadamia nuts too finely, or they could burn in the oven.

Topping

1 cup old-fashioned (rolled) oatmeal

½ cup packed light brown sugar

½ cup all-purpose flour

1 cup (4 ounces) coarsely chopped macadamia nuts

8 tablespoons (1 stick) unsalted butter

Filling

1 cup granulated sugar

1 tablespoon cornstarch

10 ripe mangoes, peeled, pitted, and cut into ½-inch thick slices (see Note)

Grated zest of 1 lime

2 tablespoons fresh lime juice

3 tablespoons unsalted butter, thinly sliced

½ gallon vanilla ice cream, for serving

1. Position a rack in the center of the oven and preheat to 350°F. Lightly butter a 13 × 9-inch baking dish.

2. To make the topping, mix the oatmeal, brown sugar, and flour with your fingers in a medium bowl, being sure to break up the sugar. Mix in the nuts. Add the butter and work it in with your fingers until the mixture is combined and crumbly. (The topping can be prepared up to 8 hours ahead and kept at room temperature.)

(continued)

3. To make the filling, whisk the sugar and cornstarch in a large bowl to combine. Add the mangoes, lime zest, and juice, and mix gently. Add the butter.
Pour into the baking dish. Sprinkle the topping evenly over the fruit.

4. Bake until the juices are bubbling and the topping is crisp, about 40 minutes.
If the nuts threaten to burn, loosely cover the crisp with aluminum foil. Cool for
at least 10 minutes before serving hot, warm, or cooled to room temperature.
(The crisp can be made up to 4 hours ahead.)

Note: To peel a mango, place the fruit on the work surface where it will balance itself. As the
mango lies on the counter, the pit runs horizontally through the center of the fruit. Don't cut vertically into the fruit, or you'll run into the pit. Turn the mango over and cut off the top of the fruit, coming just above the top of the pit. Turn the mango over and cut off the other side of the fruit. Using
a large metal serving spoon, scoop the mango flesh from each portion in one piece. The peeled
mango can now be sliced. Pare the pit portion with a small knife, and eat the flesh from the pit as
your treat.

A Father's Day Cookout Shopping List

Serves 8

Dairy

Unsalted butter (1 stick, plus 5 tablespoons)

Sharp Cheddar cheese (6 ounces, 1½ cups shredded)

Parmesan cheese (2 ounces, ½ cup freshly grated)

Dried Herbs and Spices

Chili powder (¼ cup)

Frozen

Vanilla ice cream (½ gallon)

Groceries

Anchovy paste (2 teaspoons)

Apple juice (⅓ cup, if not using bourbon)

Chili sauce, American-style (two 12-ounce jars)

Macadamia nuts (4 ounces, for 1 cup coarsely chopped)

Mayonnaise (1½ cups)

Molasses, unsulfured (½ cup)

Mustard, spicy brown (⅔ cup)

Oatmeal, old-fashioned (1 cup)

Pinto beans (four 15- to 19-ounce cans)

Sugarless peach fruit spread (two 10-ounce jars)

Tortilla chips (one 12-ounce bag)

Liquor

½ cup bourbon (or use apple juice)

Meat

Baby back pork ribs (7 pounds)

Bacon (6 slices)

Chicken breasts, boneless and skinless (two 7-ounce breasts)

Miscellaneous

Hickory chips (2 cups)

Pantry Staples

Cider vinegar (⅔ cup)

Extra virgin olive oil (2 tablespoons)

Vegetable oil cooking spray (as needed)

Worcestershire sauce (3 tablespoons)

All-purpose flour (½ cup)

Cornstarch (1 tablespoon)

Granulated sugar (1 cup)

Light brown sugar (½ packed cup)

Produce

Cabbage, Savoy (one 2¼-pound head)

Garlic cloves (1 head)

Jalapeño (2)

Lemons (3, for ⅓ cup fresh lemon juice)

Limes (2, for ¼ cup fresh lime juice and grated zest)

Mangoes (10 ripe)

Sweet onions, such as Vidalia (4 medium)

Yellow onions (1 medium)

Red bell pepper (1 small)

Scallions (1 bunch)

A Father's Day Cookout Preparation Timetable

Up to 2 weeks ahead

Make barbecue sauce; refrigerate

1 day ahead

Rub ribs with spices; wrap and refrigerate

Prepare barbecued beans; refrigerate

Make cole slaw; refrigerate

8 hours ahead

Prepare chicken breasts; chop and refrigerate

Slice mangoes; refrigerate

Prepare topping for crisp

6 hours ahead

Bake crisp; store at room temperature

4 hours ahead

Bake ribs; remove from foil

2 hours ahead

Prepare vegetables for the nachos; store at room temperature

Just as guests arrive

Assemble nachos; bake

45 minutes before serving

Bake beans

30 minutes before grilling ribs

Build charcoal fire or preheat gas grill

20 minutes before serving ribs

Unwrap ribs; grill

A Fourth of July Barbecue

For the last sixteen years, my Independence Day parties took place on my loft's rooftop terrace garden. The view stretched for miles, from the Verrazano Narrows Bridge all the way up to Riverside Church, taking

---

Serves 8

Greek Spinach and Feta Dip

Lemon Four-Pepper Chicken

Three-Bean Salad with Honey Vinaigrette

Corn with Roasted Garlic Butter

Peach-Pecan Shortcake

Herbed Iced Tea

---

in the entire Manhattan skyline. At nightfall, we could see fireworks from many different places bursting in the sky, including the display over the Statue of Liberty. The only drawback was that the roof was so perfect for daytime sunbathing, that every year, guests showed up earlier and earlier. Finally, we gave in and scheduled a daylong party that stretched late into the night. All of those good times are now a memory, as we've moved to a house, trading the roof and the view for a shady backyard.

A barbecue is truly an American institution, and as much a Fourth of July tradition as fireworks. And some of the foods are traditional, too—were corn on the cob, grilled chicken, and short-cake written into the Declaration of Independence?

The weather is usually hot, so you don't want to spend too much time in the kitchen. On the other hand, it's hard to juggle a lot of items on one grill. Bake the shortcake in the morning while the kitchen is cool. While corn can be grilled in its husk, it takes less trouble to cook it in a kettle on the stove—luckily, this happens quickly and won't steam up the kitchen too much. The spinach dip and the three-bean salad require no cooking at all, and the chicken just needs a trip to the grill. With all that time on your hands, you might be able to fit in a couple of extra innings of softball.

Greek Spinach and Feta Dip

Makes 8 to 12 servings

Make Ahead: Allow 1½ hours to drain the yogurt. The dip can be made 2 days ahead.

This tangy, attractive dip is loaded with Mediterranean flavor. I usually serve it with wedges of pita bread, but it goes well with crudités or any crisp flatbread or cracker.

1 quart plain low-fat yogurt

One 10-ounce package chopped spinach, thawed and squeezed a handful at a time to remove excess moisture

¾ cup (3 ounces) crumbled feta cheese

4 scallions, white and green parts, finely chopped

¼ cup chopped fresh dill

1 garlic clove, crushed through a press

½ teaspoon freshly ground black pepper

¼ teaspoon salt

Pita bread, cut into wedges and toasted, if desired

1. Line a wire sieve with a double thickness of rinsed, squeezed-out cheesecloth or paper towels, letting the excess cheesecloth hang over the sides. Arrange the sieve over a deep bowl and place the yogurt in the sieve. Bring up the cheesecloth to cover the yogurt and place a saucer on top. Refrigerate the whole setup until the yogurt has thickened and about 1 cup of whey has drained into the bowl, about 1½ hours.

2. Transfer the yogurt to a medium bowl. Add the spinach, feta, scallions, dill, garlic, pepper, and salt, and mix well. (For a smoother dip, process all of the ingredients in a food processor.) Cover and refrigerate to chill and blend the flavors, at least 1 hour. (The dip can be prepared 2 days ahead.)

3. Scrape the dip into a serving bowl and serve with the pita bread.

Lemon Four-Pepper Chicken

Makes 8 servings

Make Ahead: The chicken can be marinated up to 8 hours ahead.

Four-peppercorn blend—a mix of black, white, green, and pink pepper—is a staple in my spice cabinet. Of course, the peppers all look different, but they have varying flavors as well, and together they make an intriguing blend. This tangy poultry marinade (try it with swordfish, too) is a play on the popular lemon-pepper combination.

Lemon Four-Pepper Marinade

Grated zest of 2 lemons

½ cup fresh lemon juice

2 tablespoons Dijon mustard

2 tablespoons extra virgin olive oil

1 tablespoon plus 1 teaspoon four-peppercorn blend, or 2 teaspoons whole black peppercorns, coarsely crushed in a mortar and pestle or under a heavy skillet

2 garlic cloves, crushed through a press

1 teaspoon salt

Two 4-pound chickens, cut into 8 serving pieces

1. To make the marinade, mix the lemon zest and juice, mustard, oil, crushed peppercorns, garlic, and salt in a medium bowl to combine. Pour into a large self-sealing plastic bag, add the chicken, seal, and turn to coat the chicken. Refrigerate for at least 2 and up to 8 hours.

2. Meanwhile, build a charcoal fire in an outdoor grill and let burn until covered with white ash. Leave the coals heaped in a mound in the center of the grill. Do not spread out. In a gas grill, preheat on High. Turn one burner off and leave the other burner(s) on High.

3. Remove the chicken from the marinade. Lightly oil the cooking rack. Arrange the chicken around the cooler outer perimeter of the grill, not directly over the coals, and cover the grill. In a gas grill, place the chicken over the Off burner(s).

4. Cook the chicken, turning once, until it shows no sign of pink when a drumstick is pierced at the bone, about 50 minutes. Serve hot.

Three-Bean Salad with Honey Vinaigrette

Makes 8 servings
Make Ahead: The salad can be made 1 day ahead.

Three-bean salad shows up at many outdoor celebrations. The dressing is traditionally on the sugary side—my recipe uses just the right amount of honey to provide a mellow sweetness.

8 ounces green beans, trimmed and cut into 1-inch
    lengths

2 tablespoons cider vinegar

2 tablespoons honey

½ cup vegetable oil

One 15- to 19-ounce can garbanzo beans

One 15- to 19-ounce can kidney or red beans

½ cup finely chopped red onion

2 tablespoons chopped fresh parsley

Salt and freshly ground black pepper to taste

1. Bring a large pot of lightly salted water to a boil over high heat. Add the green beans and cook until they are crisp-tender, about 3 minutes. Drain, rinse under cold running water, and drain again. Pat dry with paper towels.

2. Whisk the vinegar and honey in a large bowl. Gradually whisk in the oil. Add the green beans, garbanzo and kidney beans, red onion, and parsley. Mix well. Season with the salt and pepper. Cover and refrigerate to blend the flavors, at least 1 hour. (The salad can be made 1 day ahead.) Serve chilled or at room temperature.

Corn with Roasted Garlic Butter

Makes 8 servings

Make Ahead: The garlic butter can be made 2 days ahead.

In Southern states, corn is well into its season by the Fourth (although I have to wait for another few weeks for my local crop), and the entire country seems to consider it a must-have for the Independence Day meal. Roasted garlic adds its toasty flavor to the obligatory butter. I suggest making plenty of roasted garlic butter, as most people aren't shy when it comes to hot buttered corn on the cob. Any leftover butter can be frozen for up to 2 months—add a pat to steamed vegetables or let it melt on top of a grilled steak.

2 large heads garlic

1 teaspoon olive oil, preferably extra virgin

Salt and freshly ground black pepper, as needed

1 cup (2 sticks) unsalted butter, at room temperature

8 ears of corn, husked

1. A few hours before serving, position a rack in the center of the oven and preheat to 400°F. (See Note.)

2. Using a sharp knife, cut and discard the top ½ inch off the top of a garlic head. Place the garlic head on a piece of aluminum foil. Drizzle the cut surface with ½ teaspoon oil and a sprinkle of salt and pepper. Wrap the garlic in the foil and place on a baking sheet. Repeat with the other garlic head. Bake until the garlic is tender when squeezed, about 45 minutes. Unwrap the garlic and cool completely.

3. Squeeze the soft garlic flesh out of the hulls into a small bowl. Add the butter and mash together well with a fork. (The butter can be made 2 days ahead. To freeze, scrape half of the soft butter onto a 12-inch square of wax paper. Use the wax paper to shape the butter into a 6-inch long cylinder, and wrap the butter in the paper. Freeze until solid, then overwrap with aluminum foil. Freeze for up to 2 months.)

4. Bring a large pot of water to a boil (do not add salt, which will toughen the corn). Add the corn and cook just until heated through (the water may not return to a full boil), about 5 minutes. Drain well.

5. Serve the corn hot, with the garlic butter and salt and pepper passed on the side.

Note: **You can also cook the garlic on the grill at the same time as the chicken. Place the foil-wrapped garlic on the cooler area of the grill, not over the heat, along with the chicken. It will take about 45 minutes to cook until tender.**

Peach-Pecan Shortcake

Makes 8 servings

Make Ahead: The peaches, shortcake, and whipped cream can be made up to 8 hours ahead.

Shortcake is one of the glories of summer. Whenever I serve this version, you should hear the rhapsodies—it's as if people had never had shortcake before! There are many secrets along the way to reach this perfection—a low-gluten mix of two flours, nonaluminum baking powder (which doesn't have the bitter taste of other brands), and of course the nuts. Serve it warm if possible.

Peaches

3 pounds ripe peaches, peeled, pitted, and sliced

⅓ cup packed light brown sugar, or more to taste

Shortcake

1 cup cake flour

1 cup all-purpose flour

⅓ cup granulated sugar

1 tablespoon baking powder, preferably a nonaluminum brand, such as Rumford's

¼ teaspoon salt

½ cup (2 ounces) coarsely chopped pecans

8 tablespoons (1 stick) unsalted butter, chilled, cut into ½-inch cubes

⅔ cup milk, as needed

Whipped Cream

1 cup heavy cream

2 tablespoons confectioners' sugar

½ teaspoon vanilla extract

1. At least 4 hours before serving, prepare the peaches. Stir the peaches and brown sugar in a medium bowl. Cover and refrigerate until the peaches give off their juices, at least 4 hours and up to 8 hours.

2. To make the shortcake, position a rack in the center of the oven and preheat to 375°F. Have ready a 9-inch nonstick cake pan, or butter and flour a regular pan.

3. Pulse the cake and all-purpose flours, sugar, baking powder, and salt in a food processor fitted with the metal blade just to combine. Add the pecans and pulse about 10 times until the pecans are very finely chopped, but not a powder. Add the butter and pulse 8 to 10 times until the mixture resembles coarse

crumbs with some pea-sized pieces of butter. Transfer to a medium bowl. Stirring with a fork, mix in enough of the milk to make a soft dough. (To make by hand, chop the pecans until very fine. Whisk the flours, sugar, and salt in a medium bowl. Stir in the finely chopped pecans. Cut in the butter with a pastry blender, then stir in the milk.) Knead the dough in the bowl a few times just until smooth. Do not overwork the dough. Pat the dough evenly into the cake pan.

4. Bake until the shortcake is golden brown, 25 to 30 minutes. Transfer to a wire cake rack and cool in the pan for 10 minutes. Remove from the pan. (The shortcake can be made up to 8 hours ahead, cooled, loosely covered, and stored at room temperature.)

5. To make the whipped cream, whip the cream, sugar, and vanilla in a chilled medium bowl with an electric mixer on high speed until the cream is stiff. Refrigerate until ready to serve. (The whipped cream can be prepared up to 8 hours ahead.)

6. Using a serrated knife, cut the warm shortcake into 8 wedges. Place each shortcake wedge in a dessert bowl. Top with equal amounts of the peaches and a large spoonful of whipped cream. Serve immediately.

Note: Peaches are a glorious fruit, but if you use them in baked goods, they should be peeled. It's an easy chore—as long as you start with ripe, yielding-to-the-touch peaches. Bring a pot of water to a boil over high heat and, a few at a time, add the peaches. Cook them just until their skins loosen, about 30 seconds. If the peaches aren't ripe enough, the skins will still not loosen. Don't cook the peaches longer than 1 minute, or the flesh will soften. Using a slotted spoon, transfer the peaches to a bowl of cold water and let them stand until easy to handle. Using a small paring knife, peel the peaches, or pare the ones with stubborn skins.

Some kitchenware shops now carry special peelers with very thin serrated blades that allow the cook to peel peaches (and tomatoes) without the blanching step.

Herbed Iced Tea

Makes 2½ quarts, 10 to 12 servings
Make Ahead: The tea can be made up to 1 day ahead.

This method of making iced tea couldn't be easier—no waiting for the boiled water to cool down. Herbs, such as mint or lemon verbena, infuse another layer of refreshing flavor into the tea. So that everyone can sweeten the tea to taste, serve superfine sugar alongside—regular granulated sugar won't dissolve properly.

12 large sprigs fresh mint or lemon verbena, plus more for serving

12 orange pekoe tea bags

1. Crush the mint and place in a serving pitcher. Add the tea bags and 2½ quarts cold water. Cover and let stand in a sunny place until the tea is strong, at least 3 and up to 6 hours. Remove the tea bags and mint (you can strain the tea into another pitcher, or simply fish them out with a wire strainer), pressing hard on the bags to extract any retained tea. (The strained tea can be made 1 day ahead, covered, and refrigerated.)

2. Pour the tea into tall glasses filled with ice cubes and serve chilled, adding an additional sprig of fresh mint to each serving.

A Fourth of July Barbecue Shopping List

Serves 8

Dairy

Unsalted butter (3 sticks)

Crumbled feta cheese (3 ounces)

Heavy cream (1 cup)

Milk (⅔ cup, as needed)

Plain low-fat yogurt (1 quart)

Dried Herbs and Spices

1 tablespoon, plus 1 teaspoon four-peppercorn
   blend, or 2 teaspoons black peppercorns

Frozen

Chopped spinach (one 10-ounce package)

Groceries

Garbanzo beans (one 15- to 19-ounce can)

Kidney or red beans (one 15- to 19-ounce can)

Honey (2 tablespoons)

Pecans (2 ounces)

Pita bread (1 package)

Orange pekoe tea bags (12)

Meat

Chickens, cut up (2)

Pantry Staples

Dijon mustard (2 tablespoons)

Extra virgin olive oil (2 tablespoons, plus
   1 teaspoon)

Vegetable oil (½ cup)

Cider vinegar (2 tablespoons)

Confectioners' sugar (2 tablespoons)

Granulated sugar (⅓ cup)

Light brown sugar (⅓ cup packed)

All-purpose flour (1 cup)

Cake flour (1 cup)

Baking powder (1 tablespoon)

Vanilla extract (½ teaspoon)

Produce

Corn (8 ears)

Dill (1 bunch)

Garlic (3 heads)

Green beans (8 ounces)

Lemons (3 large, for ½ cup fresh juice and
   grated zest)

Mint (1 bunch)

Parsley (1 bunch)

Peaches (3 pounds ripe)

Red onion (1 small)

Scallions (4)

A Fourth of July Barbecue Preparation Timetable

2 days ahead

Make dip; refrigerate

Make garlic butter; refrigerate

1 day ahead

Make three-bean salad; refrigerate

Make iced tea; refrigerate

8 hours ahead

Marinate and refrigerate chicken

Bake shortcake

Slice peaches; refrigerate

Whip cream; refrigerate

1 ½ hours before serving

Build fire in grill

1 hour before serving

Grill chicken

Just before serving

Cook corn

Chicken Fajita Nachos,
page 130

Hickory-Smoked Baby Back Ribs with Vidalia Onion Sauce, page 132

Lemon Four-Pepper Chicken, page 144;
Herbed Iced Tea, page 150

Peach-Pecan Shortcake,
page 148

Pork Tenderloin Tonnato, page 155; Rice, Cherry Tomato, and Basil Salad, page 157

Lemon Mousse and
Blueberry Parfaits, page 159

Grilled Eggplant and Ricotta Salata Sandwiches, page 166; Heirloom Tomato and Fresh Corn Salad, page 168

Frozen Melon Balls with Port Wine Syrup, page 169

An Alfresco Supper

The summer brings many opportunities for outdoor dining, but not all of these meals take place in the comfort of the backyard patio or apartment terrace. Often, the meal is transported to the beach or a concert in the

Serves 8

*Assorted Cheeses and Salami with Crusty Bread**

Pork Tenderloin Tonnato

Rice, Cherry Tomato, and Basil Salad

Skillet-Roasted Asparagus

Lemon Mousse and Blueberry Parfaits

*Recipe not provided

park. Alfresco suppers can be very sophisticated affairs, with lace tablecloths laid over picnic blankets and set with fine china and even silver candelabras. Therefore, my point of departure here is a grown-up meal with Mediterranean flavors. If you are also serving kids, add some grilled or fried chicken to the menu, and they will be very happy.

When the meal has to travel, the dishes must be chosen with care. They should be easy to pack and keep cold, and be equally simple to serve at the site. Instead of a prepared appetizer, I suggest simple antipasti of sliced salami, a selection of olives, and a couple of cheeses, such as a creamy Taleggio and a sharp Provolone. These items are easy to tuck into the nooks and crannies of a jammed cooler. Serve with crusty bread and refreshingly chilled white wine, and you have the perfect beginning to an outdoor supper, especially if the performance is an Italian opera. Don't forget a serving tray for the antipasti, and a cutting board and serrated knife for the bread.

An entire platter of pan-roasted pork with tuna mayonnaise, topped with capers and herbs, can be laid on the top layer of food in the cooler, and just needs to be unwrapped and sprinkled with herbs to serve. Simply prepared side dishes go perfectly with the robust tuna mayonnaise. A crisp chilled Pinot Grigio or Sauvignon Blanc would go down very well with this menu. For dessert, individual lemon mousses with blueberries, each in their own clear plastic cup, couldn't be easier to bring along, and finish the meal with style. They are especially delicious when eaten by the light of fireworks bursting overhead.

Pork Tenderloin Tonnato

Makes 8 to 10 servings

Make Ahead: The dish should be made a few hours ahead of serving to allow the flavors to blend. It can be made up to 1 day ahead.

In Italy, loin of veal is often prepared in a similar manner. However, a severe case of sticker shock brought me to substitute pork tenderloin, and now I prefer it to veal in this recipe. The tuna mayonnaise is delicious, especially as an accent to the mildly flavored pork, but its color isn't the prettiest—the chopped herbs and capers will considerably brighten its appearance.

Pork

Three 9-ounce pork tenderloins, trimmed of excess fat and silver membrane

½ teaspoon salt

¼ teaspoon freshly ground black pepper

1 tablespoon olive oil, preferably extra virgin olive oil

Tuna Mayonnaise

One 6-ounce can olive oil–packed tuna, drained

⅔ cup mayonnaise

1 tablespoon fresh lemon juice

1 teaspoon anchovy paste

1 garlic clove, crushed through a press

Freshly ground black pepper, to taste

2 tablespoons chopped fresh parsley, tarragon, or chives, in any combination, for garnish

2 tablespoons rinsed and drained capers, for garnish

1. Position a rack in the center of the oven and preheat to 400°F.

2. Season the pork with the salt and pepper. Heat the oil in a large ovenproof skillet over medium-high heat. Add the pork and cook, turning occasionally, until it is browned on all sides, about 8 minutes. Place the skillet with the pork in the oven. Bake until an instant-read thermometer inserted in the center of the pork reads 150°F, about 20 minutes. (The diameter of the pork may be too small for some thermometers to give an accurate reading. If necessary, rely on touch—the pork should feel firm and spring back when pressed in the thickest part.) Transfer to a carving board and cool completely.

(continued)

3. To make the tuna mayonnaise, process the tuna, mayonnaise, lemon juice, anchovy paste, and garlic in a food processor.

4. Holding the knife at a slight diagonal, cut the tenderloins into ½-inch-thick slices. Arrange overlapping slices of pork in a deep serving dish with a lip. Spread the tuna mayonnaise over the pork. Sprinkle with the herbs and capers. Cover with plastic wrap (do not let the wrap touch the mayonnaise or it will be messy to serve) and refrigerate to chill and blend the flavors, at least 4 hours. (The dish can be prepared up to 1 day ahead. Transfer to a cooler to transport, if desired.)

5. Remove the pork from the refrigerator (or cooler) about 20 minutes before serving to lose its chill.

Rice, Cherry Tomato, and Basil Salad

Makes 8 to 10 servings
Make Ahead: The salad can be made up to 1 day ahead.

Rice salad is a colorful and tasty summer salad that deserves the same popularity here as it has in Italy, where it is a staple on restaurant antipasti tables. However, there is one important caveat: Never serve ice-cold rice salad. Starches in the rice harden when chilled, so remember to remove the salad from the refrigerator (or cooler) at least 30 minutes before serving so the rice can soften to its natural texture.

2 cups long-grain rice, preferably converted

1 pint cherry or grape tomatoes, halved

3 tablespoons white or red wine vinegar

½ teaspoon salt

⅛ teaspoon crushed hot red pepper flakes

⅔ cup extra virgin olive oil

3 tablespoons chopped fresh basil, plus more
    for garnish

1. Bring a large saucepan of lightly salted water to a boil over high heat. Add the rice and cook, uncovered, until the rice is tender, about 20 minutes. Drain in a large wire sieve and rinse under cold water; drain again. Transfer to a large bowl and add the cherry tomatoes.

2. Whisk the vinegar, salt, and hot red pepper flakes in a small bowl to combine. Gradually whisk in the oil. Pour about two-thirds of the dressing over the rice, add the basil, and mix. Separately cover and refrigerate the salad and dressing for at least 2 hours or overnight. (The salad can be made up to 1 day ahead. Transfer the salad and dressing to a cooler to transport, if desired.)

3. About 30 minutes before serving, remove the salad from the refrigerator (or cooler) and let stand to remove the chill and soften the rice. Add enough of the reserved dressing to moisten the salad. Serve garnished with more chopped basil.

Skillet-Roasted Asparagus

Makes 8 to 10 servings

Make Ahead: The asparagus can be prepared up to 1 day ahead.

Grilling and roasting are two relatively new ways that cooks have discovered to prepare asparagus. But I don't always want to turn on the oven or set up the grill. By lightly browning the spears in a skillet, then steaming them with a small amount of water, their flavor is intensified. The asparagus is wonderful dipped in the tuna mayonnaise.

4 tablespoons extra virgin olive oil, divided

2 pounds fresh asparagus, trimmed to remove woody stems

Salt and freshly ground black pepper, to taste

1. Heat 1½ tablespoons of the oil in a large nonstick skillet over medium-high heat. Spread half of the asparagus in a single layer in the skillet and cook until the undersides are lightly browned, about 2 minutes. Roll the asparagus in the skillet to turn to the opposite side and cook for another 2 minutes to brown that side.

2. Add ⅓ cup water to the skillet and cover tightly. Cook until the asparagus is just tender and the water has evaporated, about 3 minutes. Transfer to a platter. Repeat with another 1½ tablespoons oil and the remaining asparagus. Cool completely.

3. Season the asparagus with salt and pepper and drizzle on the remaining 1 tablespoon oil. (The asparagus can be prepared up to 1 day ahead, cooled, covered, and refrigerated. Transfer to a cooler to transport, if desired.) Serve at room temperature.

Lemon Mousse and Blueberry Parfaits

Makes 8 servings

Make Ahead: The lemon curd base can be made up to 3 days ahead. The parfaits can be made up to 1 day ahead, individually wrapped, and refrigerated.

Tart lemon mousse is one of the most refreshing ways to end a meal, particularly when layered with sweet blueberries. Packed in individual plastic cups, the parfaits are easy to transport in a cooler. Classic lemon mousse uses raw eggs, which is a problem in warm weather, but this version uses a cooked lemon curd with whipped cream. The recipe is very versatile; the lemon curd can be used on its own as a tangy dessert spread, and the mousse can be used as a fluffy frosting for angel food cake. If making the angel food cake on page 91, use the whites from the egg yolks in the cake batter.

6 lemons

1 tablespoon cornstarch

1¼ cups sugar

12 tablespoons (1½ sticks) unsalted butter, cut into thin slices

9 large egg yolks

1¼ cups heavy cream

1½ pints fresh blueberries

1. Grate the zest from 2 lemons and set aside. Squeeze and strain the juice from all the lemons; you should have ¾ cup juice.

2. Whisk the lemon juice and cornstarch in a medium saucepan and stir to dissolve the cornstarch. Bring to a simmer over medium heat, whisking often. Reduce the heat to low. Add the sugar and butter and whisk until the butter melts.

3. Place the egg yolks in a small bowl and whisk to combine. Gradually whisk in about half of the hot butter mixture. Pour the yolks into the saucepan and bring just to a boil, whisking constantly. Strain through a wire sieve into a small bowl to remove any cooked strands of whites. Stir in the reserved zest. Place plastic wrap directly on top of the curd and poke a few holes in the plastic with

the tip of a sharp knife. Let the lemon curd stand until cooled. Refrigerate until chilled and set, about 2 hours. (The lemon curd can be made up to 3 days ahead, covered, and refrigerated.)

4. Whip the cream with an electric mixer on high speed in a chilled medium bowl until the cream is quite stiff. Using a rubber spatula, stir about one-third of the whipped cream into the curd to lighten the mixture. Fold in the remaining whipped cream.

5. Spoon an equal amount of the berries into 8 wine glasses or parfait glasses (if transporting, use plastic glasses or preserves jars with lids). Top with the mousse. Cover each glass with plastic wrap and refrigerate until the mousse is chilled and set, at least 2 hours or overnight. (Transfer to a cooler to transport the parfaits.) Serve chilled.

Lemon Mousse Frosting Make the lemon curd using 4 lemons (½ cup juice), 2 teaspoons cornstarch, ¾ cup plus 2 tablespoons sugar, 8 tablespoons (1 stick) unsalted butter, and 6 large egg yolks. Stir in the zest of 4 lemons. Whip ¾ cup heavy cream and fold it into the curd.

An Alfresco Supper Shopping List

Serves 8

Dairy

Unsalted butter (1½ sticks)

Heavy cream (1¼ cups)

Large eggs (9)

Delicatessen

Salami and assorted cheeses, as needed

Dried Herbs and Spices

Crushed hot red pepper flakes

Groceries

Anchovy paste (1 teaspoon)

Canned tuna, preferably in olive oil (one
    6-ounce can)

Capers (2 tablespoons)

Mayonnaise (⅔ cup)

Long-grain rice, preferably converted (2 cups)

Meat

Pork tenderloins, about 9 ounces each (3)

Pantry Staples

Extra virgin olive oil (about 1 cup)

White or red wine vinegar (3 tablespoons)

Sugar (1¼ cups)

Cornstarch (1 tablespoon)

Produce

Asparagus (2 pounds)

Basil (1 bunch)

Blueberries (1½ pints)

Cherry or grape tomatoes (1 pint)

Garlic (1 head)

Lemons (7)

Parsley (1 bunch, or use tarragon and/or
    chives)

An Alfresco Supper Preparation Timetable

1 day ahead

   Make pork tenderloin tonnato; refrigerate

   Make rice salad; refrigerate

   Prepare asparagus; refrigerate

   Make lemon mousse parfaits; refrigerate

Just before serving

   Reseason salad

A Labor Day Farmers' Market Lunch

I am blessed with a profusion of daily farmers' markets, all within a short drive of my home. This can be a mixed blessing for a professional cook—I often feel like a gambling addict who lives near Las Vegas. During late summer, the stands are bursting with

Serves 6

Cool Summer Squash and Potato Soup

Grilled Eggplant and Ricotta Salata Sandwiches

Heirloom Tomato and Fresh Corn Salad

Frozen Melon Balls with Port Wine Syrup

tomatoes, corn, arugula, eggplants, peppers, zucchini, yellow squash, cantaloupe, and other farm-fresh vegetables. I haven't quite managed to learn how to make levelheaded decisions on what to bring home, especially at the end of the season when I can never be quite sure if this will be the last time that an item might be for sale this year. My routine is to hit the market early in the morning, so by 10:00 A.M. I am often looking at a kitchen counter filled with produce. More often than not, lunch at this time of year is vegetarian, or close to it.

Even when summer produce isn't the order of the day, more people are cooking with vegetables on a regular basis. The proliferation of high-quality natural food stores with a good selection of fresh produce has helped fuel this trend. So, while a farmers' market is a fun place to buy topnotch produce, it isn't the only option. More home cooks have discovered that vegetables can make hearty main courses that the whole family can enjoy. Finally, vegetables are good for you, and there are so many of them that they bring variety to daily cooking.

This particular menu was created after a particularly indulgent farmers' market shopping spree that occurred over a long Labor Day weekend. Soup, well known for its ability to use up vegetables, was certainly in order, but it was too warm to serve a hot version. I remembered the cool minestrone that I had enjoyed in Italy, and quickly cooked a pot of a light *zuppa* with summer squash, potatoes, and thyme. The main course was sandwiches of grilled eggplant and ricotta salata, made with crusty bread from my favorite baker at the market. When I saw a market stand piled high with a rainbow of heirloom tomatoes, I knew that they would have to be added to the menu. Back home, mixed with fresh corn kernels and basil, the tomatoes were turned into a salad that was as colorful as it was flavorful.

One bite of succulent honey-sweet melon convinced me that it wouldn't need much to showcase its perfect flavor—port wine syrup proved to be a terrific match. As the meal was served with a cool bottle of Beaujolais, everyone was ready for a nap in the shade after this meal...which is not such a terrible way to spend a warm summer afternoon.

Cool Summer Squash and Potato Soup

Makes 6 to 8 servings

Make Ahead: The soup is best served the same day it is made, but it can be made 2 days ahead.

In the hot Mediterranean region, cooks often serve cool soups as a refreshing appetizer (or even as the entire meal, depending on how deadening the heat is on that particular day). This chunky soup is from that tradition. It shouldn't be ice cold—if made ahead and chilled, remove the soup from the refrigerator for about an hour before serving. Be sure that the chicken broth is thoroughly degreased, as chilled chicken fat will feel gritty on the tongue.

2 tablespoons extra virgin olive oil

2 pounds summer squash (zucchini and yellow squash in any combination), scrubbed, cut lengthwise in half, then crosswise into ½-inch thick pieces

½ cup chopped shallots

5½ cups canned reduced-sodium chicken broth

2 medium baking potatoes, peeled and cut into ¾-inch cubes

1½ teaspoons chopped fresh thyme or 1 teaspoon dried thyme

1 large ripe tomato, seeded and cut into ½-inch cubes

Salt and freshly ground black pepper to taste

1. Heat the oil in a large pot over medium heat. Add the squash and cook, stirring occasionally, until the squash is lightly browned, about 15 minutes. Add the shallots and cook until softened, about 3 minutes.

2. Add the broth, potatoes, and thyme, and bring to a boil. Reduce the heat to low and partially cover the pot with the lid. Simmer until the potatoes are tender, about 25 minutes. Add the tomato and cook just until heated through (it should retain its shape), about 3 minutes. Cool to room temperature. (The soup can be made 2 days ahead, cooled, covered, and refrigerated. Let stand at room temperature for 1 hour before serving.)

3. Just before serving, season with the salt and pepper. Ladle into soup bowls and serve.

Grilled Eggplant and Ricotta Salata Sandwiches

Makes 6 sandwiches

Eggplant has a substantial, almost meaty texture that makes it a great sandwich filling. These sandwiches, hot from the grill, have other layers of flavor beyond the eggplant itself. (Cook the eggplant and toast the bread in a broiler, if you wish.) Crusty sourdough bread is a must, and peppery arugula and sun-dried tomato pesto are much more interesting than lettuce and mayonnaise. Ricotta salata is a firm, sliceable version of the soft cheese, but you can substitute Fontina if you wish. Ricotta salata and sun-dried tomato pesto can be found at specialty grocers, Italian delicatessens, and many supermarkets. I've provided a recipe for the pesto if you want to make your own.

1 large (1½ pounds) eggplant, top trimmed

1 teaspoon salt

Extra virgin olive oil, as needed

12 slices crusty sourdough bread (cut from a wide loaf)

1 cup Sun-Dried Tomato Pesto (recipe follows), or use store-bought

6 ounces ricotta salata cheese, cut into ¼-inch-thick slices

1 bunch arugula, well rinsed and dried

1. Using a serrated knife, slice the eggplant crosswise into 12 to 14 rounds about ½ inch thick. Place the eggplant in a colander, sprinkling with the salt. Let stand in a sink to drain for 30 minutes to 1 hour. Rinse the eggplant quickly under cold water to remove the salt. Pat dry with paper towels.

2. Meanwhile, build a charcoal fire in an outdoor grill and let burn until the coals are covered with white ash and they are medium-hot (you should be able to hold your hand just above the grate for 3 seconds). For a gas grill, preheat on High, then reduce the heat to Medium.

3. Lightly oil the grill. Lightly brush both sides of the eggplant with oil. Place the eggplant on the grill and cover. Cook until the underside of the eggplant is

browned, about 4 minutes. Turn and cook until the eggplant is tender, about 4 minutes more. Transfer to a platter.

4. Place the bread slices on the grill and grill, turning once, until toasted, about 1 minute. Transfer to the platter.

5. For each sandwich, spread 2 bread slices with the pesto. Place 2 eggplant slices on 1 piece of the bread, and top with a couple of slices of ricotta salata and a few arugula leaves. Top with the second piece of bread and cut in half. Serve immediately.

Sun-Dried Tomato Pesto Process 1 cup drained and coarsely chopped oil-packed sun-dried tomatoes, ¼ cup coarsely chopped fresh basil, 3 tablespoons drained and rinsed capers, 1 garlic clove (crushed through a press), and ¼ teaspoon crushed hot red pepper flakes in a food processor. With the machine running, add ¼ cup extra virgin olive oil. Season with salt to taste. Makes about 1 cup. The pesto can be refrigerated, stored in an airtight container, with a thin layer of additional olive oil poured on top of the pesto to help preserve it, for up to 1 month.

Heirloom Tomato and Fresh Corn Salad

Makes 6 to 8 servings

Make Ahead: The salad is best served within 2 hours of making.

You won't have a wide window of opportunity to make this salad—only a few weeks in summer when both corn and tomatoes are at their peak. The corn must be sweet and fresh, as it won't be cooked, and the tomatoes must be juicy and flavorful. If you can find them, use an assortment of heirloom tomatoes, which are available in many shapes, sizes, and colors. Otherwise, good old ripe beefsteak tomatoes will do just fine.

4 large ripe tomatoes, preferably heirloom (buy a couple more tomatoes if they are small)

½ teaspoon salt, plus more as needed

2 tablespoons balsamic vinegar

½ cup extra virgin olive oil

2 cups fresh corn kernels, cut from 4 to 5 ears of corn (see Note)

¼ cup chopped fresh basil

Freshly ground black pepper, to taste

1. Using a serrated knife, cut each tomato in half lengthwise. Using your finger, poke out the seed pockets, Cut the tomatoes into ¾-inch cubes. Toss the tomatoes ½ teaspoon with salt in a medium bowl. Let stand for 20 minutes. (This step extracts the excess juices from the tomatoes so they don't dilute the vinaigrette.) Drain the tomatoes.

2. Place the balsamic vinegar in a large bowl. Gradually whisk in the oil. Add the tomatoes, corn, and basil, and toss. Season with the salt and pepper. Serve immediately, or cover and let stand for up to 2 hours.

Note: **To remove the kernels from an ear of corn, husk the corn and pull off the silk. Cut off the pointed end of the cob and stand the cob on the cut end. Using a sharp knife, cut down the cob where it meets the kernels.**

Frozen Melon Balls with Port Wine Syrup

Makes 6 servings

This dessert is best made with very sweet, almost too-ripe melon, as food loses a bit of its sweetness when frozen. It's an acceptable tradeoff, because the frozen melon balls are refreshingly cool and are like a sorbet made by Mother Nature herself. Just about any musk-type melon (those with weblike markings on their skin, such as canary or honeydew) can substitute for cantaloupe—a combination of two or three tastes and looks terrific, if you have a selection on hand. Don't use vintage port for the syrup—a modest California brand is fine.

1 large ripe cantaloupe

2 cups tawny or ruby port

¼ cup plus 2 tablespoons packed light brown sugar

Mint sprigs, for garnish

1. Using a sharp knife, cut the cantaloupe in half and scoop out the seeds. Using a melon baller, scoop out balls of melon. Spread the melon balls on a tray and freeze for at least 1 and up to 3 hours. The melon balls should be ice cold and a little frosty.

2. Bring the port and brown sugar to a boil in a medium saucepan over high heat. Cook until the mixture is syrupy and reduced to ¾ cup, 10 to 15 minutes. Transfer to a medium bowl set in a larger bowl of ice water. Let stand until the syrup is cool, about 20 minutes. Cover and refrigerate the syrup until ready to serve.

3. Divide the frozen melon balls among 6 wineglasses and top each with 2 tablespoons of the syrup. Garnish with mint sprigs and serve immediately.

A Labor Day Farmers' Market Lunch Shopping List

Serves 6

Delicatessen
Ricotta salata (6 ounces)

Groceries
Sourdough bread, round (1 loaf, for 12 slices)

Chicken broth, reduced-sodium (5½ cups)

Sun-dried tomato pesto (1 cup; if making your
own pesto, add the ingredients to this list)

Liquor
Tawny or ruby port (2 cups)

Pantry Staples
Extra virgin olive oil (about ⅔ cup, plus more as
needed for grilling the eggplant)

Balsamic vinegar (2 tablespoons)

Light brown sugar (¼ cup plus 2 tablespoons)

Produce
Arugula (1 bunch)

Basil (1 bunch)

Cantaloupe or other musk melon, very ripe
(1 large)

Corn (5 ears, for 2 cups fresh corn kernels)

Eggplant (1 large)

Mint (1 bunch)

Baking potatoes (2 medium)

Shallots (3, for ½ cup chopped)

Summer squash, such as zucchini and yellow
squash (2 pounds)

Thyme (1 bunch)

Tomatoes (1 large red tomato for the soup, and
4 heirloom tomatoes of assorted colors for
the salad)

A Labor Day Farmers' Market Lunch
Preparation Timetable

This menu is intended to be prepared and served on the same day. However, as some items need to cool, cook them in the following order:

Prepare melon balls; freeze

Make soup; cool to room temperature

Make port syrup; cool in ice water, then refrigerate

Salt eggplant; drain

Salt tomato; drain

Make corn and tomato salad

Grill sandwiches

Part Four

The Holiday Season

A Halloween Party

A Traditional Thanksgiving Dinner

An Intimate Thanksgiving

Cookie Swap

A Christmas Eve Supper

A Christmas Dinner

A Holiday Cocktail Party

A Halloween Party

I came across a couple of interesting statistics the other day. It seems that Americans spend almost seven *billion* dollars on Halloween (that's a lot of candy corn and scary masks), and that Halloween parties rival those of New Year's Eve for the most popular holiday shindigs. It's really

Serves 10

Chicken Tamale Pie

Fried Rice with Zucchini, Corn, and Beans

Slaw with Radishes and Cilantro

Red Velvet Cupcakes

Sangritas

no surprise, as Halloween is all about letting loose and having a good time. At the very least, it's the kickoff to the holiday season.

The younger you are, the more you love Halloween. Most of my Halloween memories date back to elementary school. My college degree is in theater, so I had plenty of opportunity to dress up, and the special permissiveness of wearing a costume on Halloween became less interesting. I know I am in the minority, and that there are millions of adults who love Halloween just for the chance to break out of their daily routine.

Halloween parties should have some element of spookiness, but don't go overboard. Remember that your guests will be wearing costumes, masks, and/or makeup, so don't make food that is too difficult to eat or serve. Candles may be atmospheric, but they are also dangerous around people wearing cloaks and wigs.

My only nod to the grotesque in this menu is a couple of blood-red dishes. I recommend a special tomato-juice-and-tequila cocktail for the party, the sangrita—"little blood" in Spanish. (The rest of the menu fell into place after the sangrita and is not necessarily inspired by the Mexican Day of the Dead.) For a "bucket of blood" effect, you could ladle the cocktails from a small bucket instead of a punch bowl, but that's as cute as I like to get at my Halloween bashes, with the possible exception of decorating the dessert with candy worms. The rest of the menu also has a Mexican feel to complement the cocktail: tamale pie, a cilantro-flecked slaw, and vegetable fried rice with corn and beans.

Dessert is an American classic, red velvet cupcakes. They can be as red as the amount of food coloring you add to the batter. Sangrita is not the best beverage to serve with dessert, so plan on having coffee (and/or milk, the perfect accompaniment to cupcakes) available.

Chicken Tamale Pie

Makes 10 servings
Make Ahead: The tamale pie can be made 1 day ahead.

Here's my lightened version of a buffet classic, made with chicken instead of ground beef. Chicken breast has a tendency to dry out with long cooking so thighs are a better choice.

3 tablespoons olive oil, divided

1 large onion, chopped

1 red bell pepper, seeded and chopped into ½-inch dice

1 green bell pepper, seeded and chopped into ½-inch dice

1 jalapeño, seeded and finely chopped

2 garlic cloves, finely chopped

3 pounds boneless and skinless chicken thighs, cut into 1-inch cubes

¼ cup all-purpose flour

2 tablespoons chili powder

2 cups reduced-sodium chicken broth

One 8-ounce can tomato sauce

One 12-ounce jar pitted green olives, drained and coarsely chopped

Salt, to taste

Topping

1½ cups canned reduced-sodium chicken broth

¾ teaspoon salt

1½ cups yellow cornmeal, preferably stone-ground

1 cup (4 ounces) shredded extra-sharp Cheddar cheese

3 tablespoons chopped fresh cilantro, for garnish

1. To make the filling, position a rack in the center of the oven and preheat to 350°F. Lightly oil a 13 × 9-inch baking dish.

2. Heat 2 tablespoons of the oil in a large skillet over medium-high heat. Add the onion, red and green bell peppers, jalapeño, and garlic. Cook, stirring often, until the vegetables soften, about 8 minutes. Transfer the vegetables to a bowl.

3. Heat the remaining tablespoon of oil in the skillet. In batches, add the chicken and cook, turning occasionally, until lightly browned, about 5 minutes. Add the chicken to the bowl of vegetables.

4. Return the chicken and vegetables to the skillet. Add the flour and chili powder, and stir for 30 seconds. Stir in the broth and tomato sauce, scraping up the

browned bits in the skillet, and bring to a simmer. Reduce the heat to low and simmer until the sauce is slightly thickened, about 5 minutes. Stir in the the olives. Season with salt. Spread the filling in the dish.

5. To make the topping, bring the broth and salt to a boil in a heavy-bottomed medium saucepan over high heat. Whisk the cornmeal and 1½ cups cold water together in a medium bowl, then whisk into the boiling broth. Reduce the heat to medium and cook, whisking often, until the cornmeal is very thick. Spread the cornmeal as evenly as possible on the filling—it will be a thin layer, but it will puff when baked. (The tamale pie can be made 1 day ahead, cooled, covered, and refrigerated. Remove from the refrigerator 1 hour before baking.)

6. Place the baking dish on a large baking sheet. Bake, uncovered, until the filling is bubbling, about 40 minutes (or about 50 minutes if the pie was refrigerated). Sprinkle with the cheese and bake until it melts, about 5 minutes more. Let the pie stand for 10 minutes, then garnish with cilantro and serve.

Fried Rice with Zucchini, Corn, and Beans

Makes about 10 servings

Make Ahead: The rice can be prepared up to 1 day ahead. The vegetables can be sautéed up to 2 hours ahead. The fried rice is best served right after making.

Rice is an excellent side dish, but can be difficult to make ahead and reheat for a party. However, cold rice can be sautéed with vegetables in only a few minutes and served piping hot with no loss of quality. Note that the rice must be chilled or it will clump together, so plan ahead and make it a day before serving.

2 cups long-grain rice, preferably converted

½ teaspoon salt, plus more to taste

4 tablespoons extra virgin olive oil, divided

2 medium zucchini, cut into ½-inch dice

8 scallions, white and green parts, chopped, plus
   additional for garnish

2 garlic cloves, crushed through a press

2 cups fresh or thawed frozen corn kernels

Two 15- to 19-ounce cans pinto beans, drained and
   rinsed

1½ cups canned reduced-sodium chicken broth, divided

Freshly ground black pepper, to taste

1. At least 4 hours and up to 1 day before serving, make the rice. Bring the rice, 4 cups water, and ½ teaspoon salt to a boil in a medium saucepan over high heat. Reduce the heat to low and cover tightly. Simmer until the liquid has evaporated and the rice is tender, about 18 minutes. Remove from the heat and let stand for 5 minutes. Fluff the rice with a fork and transfer to a large bowl. Cool to room temperature. Cover and refrigerate until the rice is well chilled, at least 4 and up to 24 hours.

2. Heat 2 tablespoons of the oil in a large skillet over medium-high heat. Add the zucchini and cook, stirring occasionally, until the zucchini is crisp-tender, about 5 minutes. Add the scallions and garlic and stir until the scallions are wilted, about 1 minute. Add the corn, beans, and ½ cup of the broth. Cook until the corn and beans are heated through, about 3 minutes. Transfer to a plat-

ter. (The vegetables can be prepared up to 2 hours ahead, loosely covered, and kept at room temperature.)

3. Heat the remaining 2 tablespoons oil in a large Dutch oven over medium-high heat. Add the rice and remaining 1 cup broth, and cook, stirring often to break up the clumps of rice, until it is hot, about 3 minutes. Add the vegetables and the remaining broth, and stir until everything is heated through, about 2 minutes. Season with salt and pepper.

4. Transfer to a serving bowl. Garnish with scallions and serve immediately.

Slaw with Radishes and Cilantro

Makes 10 servings

Make Ahead: The slaw is best served the day it is made, but it can be made up to 1 day ahead.

I first enjoyed a slaw like this one as a side dish to a taco in northern Mexico. While the perfect partner to the tamale pie, it can be served as a side dish to other Mexican main courses, like spicy grilled chicken or pork chops.

3½ pounds green cabbage, thinly sliced (use the slicing blade of a food processor)

About 20 large radishes, trimmed and shredded (use the large holes of a box grater or the shredding blade of a food processor)

10 scallions, white and green parts, trimmed and chopped

1 cup chopped cilantro

⅓ cup sherry vinegar or unseasoned rice vinegar

1 jalapeño, seeds and ribs removed, coarsely chopped

2 garlic cloves, smashed under a knife

1 cup olive oil

1 cup sour cream

Salt and freshly ground black pepper, to taste

1. Mix the cabbage, radishes, scallions, and cilantro in a large bowl.

2. Process the vinegar, jalapeño, and garlic in a blender to purée the jalapeño. With the machine running, add the oil through the feed tube to make a smooth dressing. Stir into the slaw. Add the sour cream and mix well. Season with salt and pepper.

3. Cover and refrigerate until well chilled, at least 4 hours. (The slaw can be made up to 1 day ahead.) Serve chilled.

Chile Peppers

When I first started writing recipes, the only relatively hot chile pepper available to the home cook was canned green chile. Then fresh jalapeños hit the market, where they had little competition for quite a few years. Now my local supermarket (and I am not talking about a gourmet superstore) also carries cherry, cayenne, and habanero chiles, and others make occasional guest appearances.

Maybe my palate has changed over the years, but it seems to me that jalapeños aren't as hot as they used to be. Have growers genetically altered the chiles to make them milder? In any case, there is a trick to turn up the heat in dishes that use chiles without having to chop up another chile pepper.

Because the heat is concentrated in the seeds and ribs, most recipes call for removing these two components before chopping the chile flesh. Do the same, but don't throw them away. Put them aside until you've tasted the dish with the chile flesh alone. If the food needs more spice, stir in the reserved seeds. If after another test the dish is still bland, mince the ribs and add them, too.

Red Velvet Cupcakes

Makes 16 cupcakes
Make Ahead: The cupcakes can be made 1 day ahead.

Recently, my friend Cynthia Stahl begged me to track down a recipe for her favorite childhood dessert, Red Velvet Cake, which seems to have been invented in the mid-1950s. There are many versions of this tender cake with a mild chocolate flavor, and they all get their ruby-red color from food coloring—some recipes call for an entire bottle! I tried substituting beet juice to get a natural red color, but the murky results were a total failure. You could leave out the coloring, but then you wouldn't have blood-red cupcakes. I prefer food-coloring paste, available at most kitchenware stores, to the liquid food coloring because it colors the batter a deeper red. The cupcake is topped with gummy candies in the shape of worms, bugs, and other gross things that will bring out the kid in you.

Cupcakes

2½ cups all-purpose flour

3 tablespoons unsweetened cocoa powder (not Dutch-processed)

1 teaspoon baking soda

½ teaspoon salt

1 cup buttermilk or ⅔ cup plain low-fat yogurt mixed with ⅓ cup milk

1 tablespoon cider or red wine vinegar

1 teaspoon vanilla extract

1 teaspoon red food-coloring paste or 2 tablespoons liquid red food coloring

8 tablespoons (1 stick) unsalted butter, at room temperature, cut into pieces

1½ cups sugar

2 large eggs, at room temperature

Frosting

⅔ cup heavy cream

5 ounces bittersweet or semisweet chocolate, finely chopped

Assorted gummy worms and bugs, for decorating the cupcakes

1. To make the cupcakes, position a rack in the center of the oven and preheat to 350°F. Line 16 muffin tins (you will use 2 muffin pans with 12 indentations each) with paper cupcake liners, staggering the liners in the tins so they are somewhat evenly distributed. (In other words, don't put all of the liners on one side of the muffin pan or the cupcakes could bake unevenly.)

2. Sift the flour, cocoa, baking soda, and salt together. Mix the buttermilk, vinegar, vanilla, and food coloring in a glass measuring cup.

3. Beat the butter in a medium bowl with an electric mixer on high speed until creamy, about 1 minute. Gradually add the sugar and beat until the mixture is very light in color with a sandy texture, about 3 minutes. One at a time, beat in the eggs. On low speed, in three additions, beat in the flour, alternating with two additions of the buttermilk, beating well after each addition and scraping down the bowl as needed with a rubber spatula. Fill each muffin tin about three-fourths full with the batter.

4. Bake until the cupcakes spring back when lightly pressed in the centers, 18 to 20 minutes. Cool for 5 minutes. Remove the cupcakes from the tins, transfer to wire cake racks, and cool completely.

5. To make the frosting, bring the heavy cream to a simmer in a medium saucepan over high heat. Remove from the heat and add the chocolate. Let stand for 3 minutes to melt the chocolate, then whisk until smooth. Transfer to a medium bowl. Cool until the chocolate mixture is as thick as chocolate pudding.

6. Using a wire whisk or an electric mixer on medium speed, whip the chocolate mixture just until it is light and fluffy. Do not overbeat or the frosting will be grainy. Spread the icing over the cupcakes and top with the candies. (The cupcakes can be prepared 1 day ahead, and stored in an airtight container at room temperature.)

Sangritas

Makes about 10 cocktails

Make Ahead: The tomato juice mixture can be prepared up to 1 day ahead.

Sangrita ("little blood" in Spanish) is served as a chaser to tequila shots in Mexico and in bars elsewhere that know a good thing when they taste one. Tomato juice provides the blood connection, with citrus juices, onion, and chile adding even more flavor. Rather than serving the tequila on the side, you can mix it with the sangrita for a terrific cocktail. I give directions for making the drinks one at a time, but you can mix sangritas in a punch bowl and serve them over ice.

1 cup orange juice, preferably freshly squeezed

¼ cup lime juice

½ cup chopped onion

1 jalapeño, seeded and chopped

One 46-ounce can tomato juice

About 2 cups gold tequila

Ice cubes, for serving

Lime wedges, for serving

1. Purée the orange juice, lime juice, onion, and jalapeño in a blender. Transfer to a large pitcher. Stir in the tomato juice. Cover and refrigerate until well chilled, at least 2 hours or overnight. (The tomato juice mixture can be made up to 1 day ahead.)

2. For each serving, fill a glass with ice cubes. Add about 3 tablespoons tequila and ¾ cup tomato juice and stir. Add a squeeze of lime and serve.

Chicken Tamale Pie,
page 176

Red Velvet Cupcakes,
page 182

Farmhouse Roast Turkey
with Rosemary Gravy,
page 192

Sweet Potato–Pineapple
Pie, page 204

A Halloween Party Shopping List

Serves 10

Dairy

Unsalted butter (1 stick)

Buttermilk (1 cup)

Cheddar cheese, extra-sharp (4 ounces)

Heavy cream (⅔ cup)

Large eggs (2)

Orange juice, freshly squeezed (1 cup)

Sour cream (1 cup)

Dried Herbs and Spices

Chili powder (2 tablespoons)

Frozen

Cut corn (2 cups frozen, or use 2 cups fresh
corn kernels from 4 to 5 ears)

Groceries

Candy, such as gummy worms (as needed,
for decorating cupcakes)

Chicken broth, canned reduced-sodium
(5 cups)

Chocolate, bittersweet or semisweet
(5 ounces)

Cocoa, unsweetened, not Dutch-processed
(3 tablespoons)

Cornmeal (1½ cups)

Paper cupcake liners (12 each)

Pitted green olives (one 12-ounce jar)

Pinto beans (two 15- to 19-ounce cans)

Red food coloring (1 teaspoon paste or
2 tablespoons liquid)

Long-grain rice, preferably converted (2 cups)

Tomato juice (one 46-ounce can)

Tomato sauce (one 8-ounce can)

Liquor

Gold tequila (2 cups, as needed)

Meat

Chicken thighs, boneless and skinless
(3 pounds)

(continued)

Pantry Staples

Extra virgin olive oil ($\frac{1}{4}$ cup)

Sherry vinegar or unseasoned rice vinegar
($\frac{1}{3}$ cup)

Cider or red wine vinegar (1 tablespoon)

Olive oil (1 cup plus 3 tablespoons, or use
extra virgin oil)

All-purpose flour ($2\frac{3}{4}$ cups)

Sugar ($1\frac{1}{2}$ cups)

Baking soda (1 teaspoon)

Vanilla extract (1 teaspoon)

Produce

Green cabbage ($3\frac{1}{2}$ pounds)

Cilantro (2 bunches)

Garlic (1 head)

Green bell pepper (1)

Jalapeños (3)

Limes (2, for $\frac{1}{4}$ cup fresh juice, plus as needed
to garnish sangritas)

Yellow onions (1 large and 1 small)

Radishes (about 20 large)

Red bell pepper (1)

Scallions (18)

Zucchini (2 medium)

A Halloween Party Preparation Timetable

1 day ahead

Make tamale pie: refrigerate

Prepare rice; refrigerate

Make cole slaw, if desired

Bake cupcakes; cool and decorate

Make tomato juice mixture for sangritas

2 hours ahead

Sauté vegetables for fried rice

Just before serving

Finish fried rice

A Traditional Thanksgiving Dinner

At most Thanksgiving gatherings, the dinner menu is set in stone, year after year: roast turkey, stuffing, gravy, cranberry sauce, some kind of potatoes (mashed, sweet, or both), and a

---

Serves 12

Sparking White Sangria Salad

Farmhouse Roast Turkey with Rosemary Gravy

Sausage and Vegetable Stuffing

Mashed Honey-Roasted Yams

Gingered Cranberry Sauce

Broccoli and Baby Carrots with Toasted Almonds

Potato and Cremini Mushroom Mash (page 259)

Sweet Potato–Pineapple Pie

---

green vegetable (at least at my table they are truly green and not drab from overcooking). Of course, there are regional variations (New Englanders often serve mashed turnips or add oysters to the stuffing) or ethnic alternations (I know many Italian families for whom the lasagna or ravioli is just as important to the meal as the bird) or family favorites (for example, my family's two-tone gelatin salad with fruit cocktail and cream cheese). No matter where you live or your heritage, you had better serve pie for dessert if you don't want disappointed guests.

As the author of three Thanksgiving-related cookbooks, I have a pretty good idea of how to get this admittedly complicated meal on the table without tears. It is all a matter of timing. I think the most important piece of advice I can share is to remove the turkey from the oven and let it stand for at least thirty minutes before carving. Not only does this allow the cooking juices to relax back into the meat and make for a juicier bird, but it gives the cook an enormous window of opportunity to reheat side dishes in the oven and make the gravy on the stove.

There are many ways to vary the menu with other recipes in the book. If you don't want mashed yams, serve the Potato and Cremini Mushroom Mash on page 259. Or substitute the Pumpkin Tart with Hazelnut Crust on page 223 for the sweet potato pie. Or serve Broccoli with Pine Nuts (page 261) instead of the baby carrots and broccoli.

This menu does not hold any earth-shattering surprises. But it does supply an abundant amount of traditional holiday flavors and aromas (Is there any scent more comforting than that of a roasting turkey?) and subsequent sensory memories. As I have said many times, the most important ingredient in a Thanksgiving menu is nostalgia.

Sparkling White Sangria Salad

Makes 12 servings

Make Ahead: The salad can be made 1 day ahead.

I only serve gelatin salad one day a year, and this one always gets raves. It's not only beautiful, but a light and refreshing appetizer to an otherwise filling meal. Use a moderately priced California or Washington Riesling, or all white grape juice for a nonalcoholic version.

2 envelopes unflavored gelatin

1½ cups Riesling wine, divided

1½ cups white grape juice

¼ cup sugar

1½ cups orange segments (cut from 2 navel oranges)

1 cup seedless green grapes, cut in halves lengthwise

½ pint fresh raspberries

1. Spray a 6-cup decorative mold with nonstick cooking spray or lightly oil the mold with vegetable oil. Sprinkle the gelatin over ½ cup of the wine in a small bowl. Let stand until the gelatin softens and swells, about 5 minutes.

2. Meanwhile, bring the remaining 1 cup wine, the grape juice, and the sugar to a boil in a medium nonaluminum saucepan over medium heat. Remove from the heat and add the gelatin mixture. Stir constantly to dissolve the gelatin completely, 1 to 2 minutes. Transfer to a medium bowl set in a larger bowl of ice water. Let stand until thickened but not set (a spoon drawn through the mixture will cut a path); 20 to 30 minutes. Whisk to create tiny bubbles in the mixture. Fold in the oranges, grapes, and raspberries. Spoon into the prepared mold and cover with plastic wrap. Refrigerate until set, at least 4 hours or preferably overnight. (The salad can be made 1 day ahead.)

3. To serve, dip the mold into a bowl of warm water for 5 seconds. Dry the outside of the mold with a kitchen towel. Moisten a serving platter with cold water (this makes it easier to move the mold on the platter if necessary). Uncover the mold and run your finger (not a knife, which could cut into the gelatin) around the inside edge of the salad to break the seal. Place the platter over the mold, hold together, and invert with a sharp shake to unmold the salad. Serve chilled.

Farmhouse Roast Turkey with Rosemary Gravy

Makes 10 to 12 servings

Teaching my Thanksgiving cooking classes all over the country, I have roasted hundreds of turkeys over the years. The secret is to cover the breast area completely with aluminum foil, which slows down the cooking and keeps the lean breast meat from drying out. During the last hour of roasting, remove the foil, baste the bird a couple of times, and you will end up with a picture-perfect turkey. I like stuffed turkey. If you are of the unstuffed school, just loosely fill the neck and body cavities with a mixture of equal amounts of chopped onions, carrots, and celery to flavor the juices.

One 14-pound whole turkey

Sausage and Vegetable Stuffing (page 198)

2 tablespoons unsalted butter, melted, plus more as
    needed

1 teaspoon salt

½ teaspoon freshly ground black pepper

6 cups Quick Turkey Stock, as needed (page 196)

⅓ cup plus 1 tablespoon all-purpose flour

1 tablespoon chopped fresh rosemary or 1½ teaspoons
    crumbled dried rosemary

1. Position a rack in the bottom third of the oven and preheat to 325°F.

2. Remove the giblets and neck from the turkey; reserve for the homemade turkey stock. Discard the liver or save it for another use (some people like to sauté and add it to the stuffing, but I cook it for the neighbor's cat). Rinse the turkey inside and out with cold water; pat dry with paper towels. Pull off the pale yellow fat on both sides of the tail and set aside. Loosely fill the neck cavity with some of the stuffing—do not pack the stuffing. Fold over the neck skin and secure to the back skin with a metal or bamboo skewer. Loosely fill the body cavity with some of the remaining stuffing. Cover the exposed stuffing with a piece of foil. Place any remaining stuffing in a lightly buttered casserole, cover with the lid or aluminum foil, and refrigerate to bake as a side dish. Tie the ends of the drumsticks together with kitchen twine, or tuck them under the flap of skin (or

the plastic or metal "hock lock"). Lift the wing tips up and over the back and tuck them under the bird.

3. Place the turkey on a roasting rack set in a roasting pan. Add the reserved turkey fat to the pan. Brush the turkey all over with melted butter and sprinkle with the salt and pepper. Tightly cover the breast area (not the wings) with aluminum foil. Add 3 cups water to the pan. Roast, basting every 45 minutes (including the area under the foil), until an instant-read thermometer inserted in the meaty part of the thigh (not touching a bone) registers 180°F, about 4 hours. During the last hour of roasting, remove and discard the foil. As the water in the pan evaporates, add 1 cup water to keep the drippings from scorching.

4. Transfer the turkey to a large serving platter, reserving the pan drippings for sauce. Let the turkey stand uncovered for at least 30 minutes before carving. Increase the oven temperature to 350°F. Drizzle ½ cup turkey stock over the stuffing in the casserole, cover, and bake until heated through, about 30 minutes. (If you like crispy stuffing, remove the foil after 15 minutes.)

5. Meanwhile, pour the reserved pan drippings into a heatproof glass bowl or large measuring cup. Let stand for 5 minutes, then skim off and reserve the clear yellow fat that has risen to the top. Measure ½ cup fat, adding melted butter (or better yet, melt the solidified fat from the turkey stock), if needed. Add enough turkey stock to the skimmed drippings to make 6 cups total.

6. Place the roasting pan on two stove burners over medium-low heat and add the turkey fat. Whisk in the flour, scraping up the browned bits on the bottom and sides of the pan, and cook until the flour is lightly browned, about 2 minutes. Whisk in the turkey stock and rosemary. Cook over medium heat, whisking often, until the gravy has thickened and no trace of flour taste remains, about 5 minutes. Keep the gravy warm until ready to serve.

7. Pour the gravy into a warmed gravy boat. Carve the turkey and serve the gravy and stuffing alongside. *(continued)*

Estimated Turkey Roasting Times (Oven Temperature 325°F)

Allow an extra 30 minutes to the roasting time to provide for variations in roasting conditions.

Unstuffed Turkey

8 to 12 pounds	2$\frac{3}{4}$ to 3 hours
12 to 14 pounds	3 to 3$\frac{3}{4}$ hours
14 to 18 pounds	3$\frac{3}{4}$ to 4$\frac{1}{4}$ hours
18 to 20 pounds	4$\frac{1}{4}$ to 4$\frac{1}{2}$ hours
20 to 24 pounds	4$\frac{1}{2}$ to 5 hours

Stuffed Turkey

8 to 12 pounds	3 to 3$\frac{1}{2}$ hours
12 to 14 pounds	3$\frac{1}{2}$ to 4 hours
14 to 18 pounds	4 to 4$\frac{1}{4}$ hours
18 to 20 pounds	4$\frac{1}{4}$ to 4$\frac{3}{4}$ hours
20 to 24 pounds	4$\frac{3}{4}$ to 5$\frac{1}{4}$ hours

Tips for a Perfect Turkey

Get a fresh turkey There is hardly any reason for buying a frozen turkey anymore. Fresh turkeys are readily available, and they have superior flavor. I much prefer an all-natural turkey that has not been injected with artifical "butter" flavoring. Buy a fresh turkey no more than 2 days before roasting it.

Don't underestimate how much turkey to buy To ensure there will be enough meat for leftovers and seconds, allow at least 1 pound of uncooked turkey for each person. Although large tom turkeys (about 14 pounds and up) have more meat on their bones than the smaller hens, this is a good rule of thumb.

Be flexible with roasting times There are many variables that can affect the roasting time: the temperature of the turkey, inaccurate oven temperature, too frequent opening of the oven door (which drops the temperature), and even the temperature of the stuffing. Tack on an additional 30 minutes to the roasting time, just to be sure.

Use an accurate meat thermometer Do not trust the pop-up thermometers that come with many turkeys—they can become glued shut by the cooking juices. Use a meat thermometer, inserted in the thickest part of the thigh (between the thigh and the drumstick), not touching a bone, to check the temperature. I prefer the digital probe thermometer for this job because the monitor sits on the kitchen counter and gives an accurate idea of the turkey's progress as it cooks.

Let the turkey rest before carving A rest period before carving (for the turkey, not the cook) is one of the secrets to a moist, juicy bird. The hot juices in the turkey must cool and relax back into the meat—if the bird is carved too soon, they will squirt out and contribute to dry meat. The larger the bird, the longer it can stand at room temperature without cooling off. Allow 30 minutes for an average-sized bird of about 15 pounds, and up to 1 hour for large birds around 20 pounds. With the turkey on the platter, the oven is now free for reheating side dishes.

Quick Turkey Stock

Makes about 8 cups
Make Ahead: The stock can be made 1 day ahead.

The neck and giblets from the turkey can become the beginnings of a creditable stock that will add distinction to your stuffing and gravy. (Or use the bones, skin, and trimmings from boning a whole breast for the Herbed Turkey Breasts on page 216.) While a typical stock can take many hours to simmer, this one is ready in an hour or two, thanks to canned chicken broth, which boosts the stock's flavor.

1 tablespoon vegetable oil

Neck, heart, and gizzard from 1 turkey (do not use the
  liver)

1 small onion, chopped

1 small carrot, chopped

1 small celery rib with leaves, chopped

Two 14½-ounce cans reduced-sodium chicken broth

3 fresh parsley sprigs

½ teaspoon dried thyme

¼ teaspoon whole black peppercorns

1 bay leaf

1. The night before roasting the turkey, heat the oil in a large saucepan over medium-high heat. Chop the neck with a heavy knife or cleaver into 2-inch chunks (or ask the butcher to do this). Add the neck, heart, and gizzard to the pot. Cook, uncovered, turning occasionally, until the turkey parts are browned, about 7 minutes. Add the onion, carrot, and celery. Cook, stirring occasionally, until they soften, about 5 minutes.

2. Stir in the broth and enough cold water to cover the ingredients by 1 inch. Bring to a boil over high heat, skimming off any foam that rises to the surface. Add the parsley, thyme, peppercorns, and bay leaf. Reduce the heat to low and simmer, uncovered, for at least 1 and up to 2 hours.

3. Strain the stock through a colander into a large bowl, discarding the solids. Cool to room temperature. Cover and refrigerate.

4. The next day, scrape off the solidified fat from the surface of the stock. Transfer the fat to small bowl, cover, and refrigerate (use it instead of butter when making turkey gravy). Reheat the stock in a large saucepan before use.

Sausage and Vegetable Stuffing

Makes 12 servings

Make Ahead: The sausage and vegetable mixture can be prepared 1 day ahead. Assemble the stuffing just before using.

This old-fashioned stuffing features all of the flavors that people expect from a traditional dressing. Although I have more recipes than I can count, this is the one I make year after year. You will have leftover stuffing after filling the turkey—spread it in a buttered baking dish, refrigerate, then reheat as a side dish.

1 tablespoon vegetable oil

1 pound mildly spiced bulk pork sausage or turkey sausage links (remove the casings from the turkey sausage)

4 tablespoons (½ stick) unsalted butter

2 medium onions, chopped

6 medium celery ribs with leaves, chopped

1 teaspoon dried thyme

1 teaspoon dried sage

1 teaspoon dried marjoram, optional

1 teaspoon crumbled dried rosemary

½ teaspoon freshly ground black pepper

One 16-ounce package seasoned bread cubes for stuffing

⅓ cup chopped fresh parsley

1½ cups Quick Turkey Stock (page 196), as needed

1. Heat the oil in a large skillet over medium heat. Add the sausage and cook, breaking up the meat with the side of a spoon into bite-sized pieces, until the sausage is cooked through, about 8 minutes. Using a slotted spoon, transfer the sausage to a large bowl.

2. Add the butter to the skillet and melt. Add the onions and celery. Cover and cook, stirring occasionally, until the vegetables are tender, about 10 minutes. Stir in the thyme, sage, marjoram (if using), rosemary, and pepper. Return the sausage to the pan and mix well. (The sausage mixture can be prepared up to 1 day ahead, cooled, covered, and refrigerated. Reheat it in a large skillet over medium heat before proceeding.)

3. Mix the stuffing cubes, sausage mixture, and parsley in a large bowl. Gradually stir in enough turkey stock to moisten the stuffing evenly. Use immediately to stuff the turkey. Reserve the remaining stuffing to serve as a side dish. (See instructions in Farmhouse Roast Turkey, page 192.)

Mashed Honey-Roasted Yams

Makes 12 servings

Make Ahead: The yams can be prepared up to 8 hours ahead

What we call yams or sweet potatoes (the true yam and true sweet potato are entirely different) are already sweet, but roasting really brings out their sugar. I much prefer this version to any with marshmallows, but truth be known, you can spread marshmallows on top of the baked yams and broil them until the topping is nicely browned. Get someone to help you with peeling the yams.

5 pounds orange-fleshed yams, such as Louisiana, garnet, or jewel, peeled and cut into 1½-inch chunks

2 teaspoons vegetable oil

4 tablespoons (½ stick) unsalted butter

⅓ cup honey, divided

¾ teaspoon salt

1. Preheat the oven to 375°F. Spray a large baking sheet with cooking spray.

2. Mix the yams and oil in a large bowl with your hands to coat the yams lightly with oil. Spread evenly on the baking sheet. Roast, stirring occasionally, until the yams are tender, about 1½ hours.

3. Mash the yams, butter, ¼ cup honey, and salt in a large bowl with an electric mixer on high speed. (The yams can be prepared up to 8 hours ahead, cooled, covered, and refrigerated. Spread the yams in a buttered 2½-quart ovenproof serving dish and cover. Reheat in a preheated 375°F oven for 30 minutes.)

4. Transfer the yams to a serving dish, drizzle with the remaining 1 tablespoon honey, and serve hot.

Gingered Cranberry Sauce

Makes about 3 cups
Make Ahead: The cranberry sauce can be made up to 1 week ahead.

The simple addition of crystallized ginger takes good old cranberry sauce to another level. While they are in season, buy extra bags of cranberries and freeze them to make this sauce at other times of the year. It is fantastic with grilled pork chops or baked ham.

One 12-ounce bag cranberries, rinsed and picked over

1½ cups sugar

½ cup coarsely chopped crystallized ginger (available at Asian markets, specialty food stores, and many supermarkets)

1. Bring the cranberries, sugar, ginger, and ½ cup water to a boil in a medium nonaluminum saucepan over medium heat, stirring often to dissolve the sugar. Reduce the heat to medium-low. Simmer uncovered, stirring often, until all the berries have burst, about 5 minutes.

2. Transfer the sauce to a medium bowl and cool completely. (The sauce can be made up to 1 week ahead, cooled, covered, and refrigerated.) Serve at room temperature.

Broccoli and Baby Carrots with Toasted Almonds

Makes 12 servings
Make Ahead: The almonds and vegetables can be prepared 1 day ahead.

Parcooked vegetables only need a brief sauté in a large skillet at serving time. A splash of turkey stock keeps them from the sin of blandness, and almonds add crunch.

½ cup sliced natural almonds

1 pound baby-cut carrots

1 head broccoli, trimmed and cut into florets

2 tablespoons (¼ stick) unsalted butter

¼ cup chopped shallots

½ cup Quick Turkey Stock (page 196) or canned reduced-sodium chicken broth

½ teaspoon salt

¼ teaspoon freshly ground black pepper

1. Heat an empty medium skillet over medium heat. Add the almonds and cook, stirring often, until toasted, about 3 minutes. Transfer the almonds to a small bowl, cover tightly, and set aside. (The almonds can be prepared 1 day ahead and stored at room temperature.)

2. Bring a large pot of lightly salted water to a boil over high heat. Add the carrots and cook until barely tender, about 7 minutes. Using a large skimmer or wire sieve, transfer the carrots to a large bowl of ice water, and cool the carrots in the water. (Keep the pot of water boiling.) Drain well. Pat the carrots dry in paper towels.

3. Add the broccoli to the water and cook until crisp-tender, about 4 minutes. Drain, rinse under cold running water, and drain well. Pat dry with paper towels. (The carrots and broccoli can be prepared up to 1 day ahead. Wrap separately in fresh paper towels, store in zippered plastic bags, and refrigerate.)

4. When ready to serve, melt the butter in a 12-inch skillet over medium heat. Add the shallots and cook, stirring occasionally, until softened, about 2 minutes.

Add the carrots, broccoli, turkey stock, salt, and pepper. Cover and cook, stirring occasionally, until the vegetables are heated through and the stock is almost evaporated, about 5 minutes.

5. Transfer the vegetables to a serving bowl, sprinkle with the toasted almonds, and serve hot.

Sweet Potato–Pineapple Pie

Makes 8 to 12 servings
Make Ahead: The pie can be made 1 day ahead.

Sweet potato pie (usually made not with the true sweet potato, which is pale yellow, but with orange-fleshed yams) graces many Southern holiday tables as a substitute for pumpkin pie. As more cooks discover American regional cooking, this spicy treat is finding its place on menus throughout the country. One pie will make 8 average-sized servings, or 12 thin slices. For 12 servings, add a scoop of vanilla ice cream to the dessert plate; I usually bake two pies, as leftover pie is always welcome. Or make one sweet potato pie and add a store-bought dessert, such as pecan pie, to the menu.

1 pound orange-fleshed yams, such as Louisiana, garnet, or jewel (sometimes called sweet potatoes)

One 9-inch pie shell (see Flaky Old-fashioned Pie Dough, page 206)

3 large eggs

½ cup packed light brown sugar (see Note)

½ cup half-and-half or light cream

One 8-ounce can crushed pineapple in juice, well drained

4 tablespoons (½ stick) unsalted butter, melted

1 teaspoon ground cinnamon

Sweetened whipped cream (page 224), for serving

1. Bring a large saucepan of lightly salted water to a boil over high heat. Add the yams and cook until tender when pierced with the tip of a knife, about 40 minutes. Drain the yams and cool until easy to handle. Peel the yams and place in a medium bowl. Mash the yams with a potato masher or an electric mixer. You should have 1½ cups mashed sweet potatoes.

2. Meanwhile, preheat the oven to 400°F. Prick the pie shell all over with a fork. Place the pie shell on a baking sheet. Line the pie shell with a piece of aluminum foil. Fill the foil with a few handfuls of aluminum or ceramic pie weights (or use dried beans). Bake until the edges of the shell look set, about 10 minutes. Lift off the foil with the pie weights. Return to the oven and bake until the shell is lightly browned, about 10 minutes more. Remove the pie shell from the oven.

3. Whisk the eggs and brown sugar in a medium bowl to dissolve the sugar. Add the mashed yams, half-and-half, pineapple, butter, and cinnamon, and whisk well to combine. Pour into the pie shell.

4. Return the pie to the oven and bake 10 minutes. Reduce the heat to 350°F. Bake until a knife inserted in the center comes out clean, about 45 minutes. Cool completely. (The pie can be prepared 1 day ahead, covered, and refrigerated.) Serve with the whipped cream.

Note: If the brown sugar isn't completely moist (hard brown sugar will not dissolve or cream well with butter), rub the sugar through a wire sieve to give it a lighter consistency.

Flaky Old-fashioned Pie Dough

Makes one 9-inch pie crust
Make Ahead: The dough can be prepared up to 2 days ahead.

While busy cooks may prefer a refrigerated or frozen piecrust (and some of them can be good), other cooks with more time may want to make their own dough. This is my tried-and-true recipe for a tender crust that would make any mom smile with pride. It uses vegetable shortening to create the flaky quality that is the benchmark of a fine American-style crust, with butter for flavor. I give detailed instructions for those who are new to pie-making.

1½ cups all-purpose flour

1 tablespoon sugar

¼ teaspoon salt

⅓ cup plus 1 tablespoon vegetable shortening, chilled, cut into ½-inch cubes

3 tablespoons unsalted butter, chilled, cut into ½-inch cubes

¼ cup ice-cold water

1 large egg yolk

½ teaspoon cider or red wine vinegar

1. In a large bowl, mix the flour, sugar, and salt until combined. Using a pastry blender, rapidly cut the shortening and butter into the flour mixture until it is the consistency of coarse bread crumbs with some pea-sized pieces. Do not blend to a fine cornmeal-like consistency. If the fats stick to the wires of the blender, scrape them off. (Or pulse the flour, sugar, and salt in a food processor to combine. Add the shortening and butter and pulse until the fat in the mixture resembles coarse bread crumbs. Transfer the mixture to a large bowl.)

2. In a glass measuring cup, mix the ice water, yolk, and vinegar. Tossing the flour mixture with a fork, gradually add the ice water mixture, sprinkling it all over the ingredients in the bowl. Mix well, being sure to moisten the crumbs on the bottom of the bowl. Add just enough liquid until the dough clumps together. It does not have to come together into one big ball. To check the consistency, press the dough between your thumb and forefinger. The dough should be

moist, but not wet and not crumbly. If necessary, gradually mix in more ice water, 1 teaspoon at a time, until you reach the correct consistency.

3. Gather up the dough into a thick disk and wrap in wax paper. (Wax paper is better than plastic wrap because plastic wrap can trap moisture in the pastry and create a sticky exterior.) Refrigerate the dough for at least 1 hour and up to 2 days. If the chilled dough is very hard, let it stand at room temperature for 10 minutes before rolling out.

4. Sprinkle the work surface lightly but completely with flour, then spread out the flour with the palm of your hand into a very thin layer. Place the dough on the work surface, then sprinkle the top of the dough with a little flour, too. Don't bother to sprinkle the rolling pin with flour—it just falls off. Starting at the center of the disk, roll the dough away from you. (If the dough cracks while rolling out, it could be too cold. Let it stand for a few minutes to warm up slightly, then try again.) Turn the dough a quarter turn. Roll out again from the center of the dough. Continue rolling out the dough, always starting from the center of the dough and turning it a quarter turn after each roll, until the dough is about 13 inches in diameter and ⅛ inch thick. (If you aren't sure what ⅛ inch looks like, stand a ruler up next to the dough and check.) Be sure that the dough is the same thickness throughout, especially at the edges, which tend to be thicker than the center. Work as quickly as possible so the dough doesn't get too warm.

5. Carefully fold the dough into quarters. If you think the dough is too warm to fold without breaking, and you have rolled out the dough on a cutting board, transfer the entire board to the refrigerator—if it's a cold day, placing it outside on a window sill or in an unheated room is fine—for a few minutes to firm up. Transfer the dough to the pie pan, with the point in the center of the pan. Unfold the dough, letting the excess dough hang over the sides of the pan. Gently press the dough snugly into the corners of the pan. (If the dough cracks, just press

the cracks together. Gaps can be patched with a scrap of dough, moistened lightly around the edges to adhere it to the crust.) Using kitchen scissors or a sharp knife, trim the dough to extend only ½ inch beyond the edge of the pan.

6. To flute the crust, fold the edge of the dough underneath itself so the folded edge is flush with the edge of the pan. Use one hand to pinch the dough around the knuckle or fingertip of your other hand, moving around the crust at 1-inch intervals. Cover the dough with plastic wrap and refrigerate or freeze until chilled, 15 to 30 minutes.

A Traditional Thanksgiving Dinner Shopping List

Serves 12

Dairy

Unsalted butter (about 2½ sticks)

Half-and-half (½ cup)

Heavy cream (1 cup, for pie)

Large eggs (4)

Dried Herbs and Spices

Bay leaf (1)

Whole black peppercorns (¼ teaspoon)

Ground cinnamon (1 teaspoon)

Dried marjoram (1 teaspoon, optional)

Dried thyme (1½ teaspoons)

Dried rosemary (1 teaspoon or 2½ teaspoons
    if using dried rosemary for gravy)

Dried sage (1 teaspoon)

Groceries

Sliced almonds (½ cup)

Chicken broth, reduced-sodium (two
    14½-ounce cans, 3½ cups if making
    Quick Turkey Stock; if not making stock,
    buy 1 quart chicken broth)

Unflavored gelatin (2 envelopes)

Crystallized ginger (½ cup, coarsely chopped)

White grape juice (1½ cups)

Honey (⅓ cup)

Crushed pineapple in juice (one 8-ounce can)

Stuffing cubes, seasoned variety (one
    16-ounce package)

Vegetable shortening (⅓ cup plus 1 tablespoon)

Liquor

Riesling wine (1½ cups)

Meat

Bulk pork sausage, mildly seasoned (1 pound)

Turkey (one 14-pound turkey)

Pantry Staples

Cider or red wine vinegar (½ teaspoon)

Vegetable oil (about 3 tablespoons)

All-purpose flour (2 cups plus 2 tablespoons)

Confectioners' sugar (1 tablespoon, for
    whipped cream)

Granulated sugar (about 3 cups)

Light brown sugar (½ cup)

Vanilla extract (1 teaspoon, for whipped cream)

Produce

Broccoli (1 head)

Baby-cut carrots (1 pound)

Carrots (1 small)

Cranberries (one 12-ounce bag)

Celery (1 small plus 6 medium)

Green seedless grapes (1 cup)

Yellow onions (2 medium plus 1 small)

Navel oranges (2)

Parsley (1 bunch)

Raspberries (½ pint)

Rosemary (1 bunch)

Shallots (2, for ¼ cup chopped)

Yams (6 pounds)

A Traditional Thanksgiving Dinner Preparation Timetable

1 week ahead

Make cranberry sauce; refrigerate

2 days ahead

Make pie dough; refrigerate

1 day ahead

Make gelatin salad; refrigerate

Make turkey stock; refrigerate

Sauté sausage and vegetables for stuffing; refrigerate

Make yams; refrigerate

Toast almonds; cover and store at room temperature

Prepare baby carrots and broccoli; refrigerate

Make sweet potato pie; refrigerate

About 5½ hours before serving (allows for preheating oven and precarving rest period for turkey)

Reheat sausage and vegetables; make stufing

Stuff and roast turkey

Whip cream for pie; refrigerate

After turkey is removed from oven

Reheat yams

Heat stuffing

Make gravy; keep warm

Just before serving appetizer

Unmold salad

Just before serving main course

Sauté baby carrots and broccoli

An Intimate Thanksgiving

Not every Thanksgiving dinner is a huge meal with relatives and friends coming out of the woodwork. Because so many people go away over the long holiday weekend, I sometimes find myself with a

---

Serves 8

Sherried Crab Bisque

Herbed Turkey Breasts with Cranberry-Merlot Sauce

Celery Root Purée

Brussels Sprout Chiffonade with Pancetta

Gingered Cranberry Sauce (page 201)

Pumpkin Tart with Hazelnut Crust

---

somewhat smaller group than the usual horde. On these occasions, the holiday meal is relaxed and intimate, shared with close friends who I know appreciate a lighter, more sophisticated menu than the typical Thanksgiving fare.

Before, when faced with a small group of Thanksgiving dinner guests, I still roasted a small turkey and insisted on making the classic endless list of trimmings. I wanted plenty of food for seconds and leftovers to pack up and send home with the guests. Invariably, almost everyone at the party had to travel over the upcoming weekend and declined the leftovers, which they wouldn't get to until Monday. So, I ended up with a mountain of leftover turkey. A new plan was obviously in order.

Now I make a meal that utilizes some of the most popular harvest-time flavors, but has more of a dinner party feel. Frankly, this menu is so versatile, I use it for dinner parties throughout the autumn and winter months. For the typical multicourse holiday meal, I would shy away from a rich appetizer like crab bisque, but it is ideal for this streamlined menu. The main course, herbed turkey breasts with a cranberry-Merlot sauce, anchors the meal with an updated approach to the holiday bird. (I say updated because twenty years ago, you would be hard pressed to find boneless turkey breast at your market, and now it is as available as hamburger, especially around the holidays.) A chiffonade of Brussels sprouts flavored with pancetta is a fresh approach to this often overlooked (and improperly overcooked) fall vegetable. Instead of the requisite holiday dish of mashed potatoes, try the purée of celery root instead. You may never go back to mashed potatoes. As much as I like it, I purposely left stuffing out of this nicely balanced menu. (I think that we could all do with fewer carbohydrates at Thanksgiving, anyway.) If you can't get through

Thanksgiving without stuffing, make a small batch of your favorite recipe and bake it in a casserole—it doesn't have to go inside of the bird. The pumpkin tart in a hazelnut crust is a wonderful twist on pumpkin pie, and comes together in no time—you don't even have to roll out the tart dough, just press it in the pan.

A simply prepared, elegant Thanksgiving meal is something to be thankful for.

Sherried Crab Bisque

Makes 8 servings

Make Ahead: The bisque can be prepared 1 day ahead and reheated. Add the crab just before serving.

One year, I made crab bisque from scratch, which entails cooking and cleaning the crabs, making a stock out of the shells, and more. It was very good, but I practically fell asleep at the dinner table from exhaustion. This was one of those times when I said to myself, "If I am a professional and it took me all day to make this, what about an untrained cook?" I swore to make an easier version that I liked just as much, and here it is. If you don't want to use sherry, just add more clam juice.

6 tablespoons (¾ stick) unsalted butter

1 large onion, finely chopped

1 medium celery rib, finely chopped

⅓ cup plus 1 tablespoon unbleached or all-purpose flour

Two 13¾-ounce cans reduced-sodium chicken broth

Two 8-ounce bottles clam juice

½ cup dry sherry

1½ tablespoons tomato paste

1 pound fresh crabmeat, picked through for cartilage and shells

¾ cup heavy cream

Salt and hot red pepper sauce, to taste

Chopped fresh parsley, for garnish

1. Melt the butter in a large saucepan over medium-low heat. Add the onion and celery and cover. Cook until the vegetables are tender but not browned, about 10 minutes. Stir in the flour. Cook, uncovered, stirring often, without browning the flour, for 1 minute.

2. Gradually whisk in the broth, clam juice, sherry, and tomato paste. Bring to a boil over high heat. Reduce the heat to low and partially cover the saucepan with the lid. Simmer, stirring often, until the bisque is lightly thickened, about 10 minutes. (The bisque can be prepared up to this point 1 day ahead, cooled, cov-

ered, and refrigerated. Reheat to simmering before proceeding. If the bisque is too thick, thin with additional chicken broth.)

3. Add the crab and the cream, increase the heat to medium, and cook just until very hot—do not boil. Season the bisque with the salt and hot sauce. Serve hot in soup bowls, sprinkling each serving with parsley.

Herbed Turkey Breasts with Cranberry-Merlot Sauce

Makes 8 servings
Make Ahead: The turkey roast can be rolled and tied up to 1 day ahead.

This simple method of preparing turkey breast infuses the meat with lots of flavor. While turkey breast roasts are easy enough to find at the market, cutting the roasts from a whole turkey breast will give you the trimmings to prepare turkey stock, which always makes the best sauce. The turkey breasts need to be butterflied, a simple enough procedure, but ask the butcher to do it, if you prefer. (If you ask nicely, I bet the butcher would bone the whole breast, too.) Two breasts will yield a reasonable amount of turkey for seconds, and perhaps leftovers.

2 boneless and skinless turkey breast roasts, about
    1½ pounds each (see page 218)

1½ tablespoons chopped fresh parsley

1½ tablespoons chopped fresh rosemary, plus sprigs for
    garnish

1½ tablespoons chopped fresh sage, plus sprigs for
    garnish

½ teaspoon salt, plus more to taste

¼ teaspoon freshly ground black pepper, plus more to
    taste

4 tablespoons (½ stock) unsalted butter, divided
    (2 tablespoons chilled)

½ cup Quick Turkey Stock (page 196), made from breast
    trimmings (see sidebar, page 218) or canned
    reduced-sodium chicken broth, as needed

½ cup Merlot or other dry red wine

½ cup (3 ounces) dried cranberries

½ teaspoon cornstarch, dissolved in 1 tablespoon water

1. Position a rack in the center of the oven and preheat to 350°F.

2. Place one turkey breast, skin side down, on a work surface. Using a sharp knife, cut a deep incision into the thickest part of the meat on one side of the roast, being careful not to cut through completely. Open this flap like a book to one side to butterfly the roast. Make a cut on the other side, being careful not to cut through completely, and fold out in the other direction. Pound the breast gently to flatten evenly. Mix the parsley, rosemary, and sage. Sprinkle half of the

herbs over the cut surface of the roast. Starting at a short end, roll the breast into a thick cylinder. Tie crosswise in a few places with kitchen string. Repeat with the second turkey breast. Season the outside of both roasts with the ½ teaspoon salt and ¼ teaspoon pepper.

3. Melt 2 tablespoons of the butter in a Dutch oven or flameproof casserole slightly larger than the two turkey breasts over medium-high heat. Add the breasts and cook, turning occasionally, until browned on all sides, about 10 minutes. Cover tightly and bake until an instant-read thermometer inserted in the center of the breast reads 165°F, 35 to 40 minutes. Transfer the turkey breasts to a carving board and cover with aluminum foil to keep warm.

4. Pour the cooking juices out of the pot into a 2-cup glass measuring cup. Let stand for a few minutes, then skim off the fat that rises to the surface. Add enough broth to the cooking juices to make 1 cup. Return the liquid to the pot and add the wine and cranberries. Bring to a boil over high heat. Boil until reduced to about ¾ cup, about 5 minutes. Whisk in the cornstarch and cook for 15 seconds, just to give the sauce a slightly heavier consistency. Remove from the heat and whisk in the chilled butter, 1 tablespoon at a time. Season the sauce with salt and pepper. Transfer to a sauceboat.

5. Remove the strings from the roasts. Cut crosswise into ½-inch thick slices. Transfer to a serving platter. Garnish with the rosemary and sage sprigs. Serve hot, with the sauce on the side. *(continued)*

Turkey Breasts

If you can't find boneless, skinless turkey breast roasts (sometimes called turkey London broil), you can bone a whole turkey breast. While I can't deny the convenience of boneless turkey, I often bone the whole breast because it is more economical. Plus I get the bones and skin to make turkey stock. While the herbed turkey breasts and Brussels sprouts recipes use a total of only 1 cup turkey stock, freeze the remaining stock. It is a great substitute for chicken stock.

Start with a whole turkey breast weighing about 5½ pounds. Using a sharp, thin knife, remove the turkey skin. With the tip of the knife scraping against the bones, working from the breastbone down to the ribs, cut off the lobe of breast meat from one side of the breast. Repeat with the other side of the breast to make two boneless, skinless turkey roasts weighing about 1½ pounds each. To use the bones for Quick Turkey Stock (page 196), chop the bones into manageable pieces with a heavy cleaver or knife. Add the skin to the stock pot, too.

Celery Root Purée

Makes 8 servings

Make Ahead: The celery root can be prepared up to 8 hours before cooking.

Celery root purée may look like mashed potatoes, but when guests take their first bite, their will faces light up with surprise. More people should know about this delicious vegetable, which is at its peak during the late autumn. The size varies, so you could need anywhere from two large roots to four smaller ones for this dish. It isn't the prettiest vegetable at the produce store—my market now sells celery root pared of its dirt-crusted, gnarly brown skin. If your celery root comes au naturel, pare it first before rinsing it, or you'll end up with mud all over your kitchen counter.

3 pounds celery root

1 pound baking potatoes, peeled and cut into 1-inch chunks (if preparing ahead, store in a bowl of cold water for up to 8 hours)

4 tablespoon unsalted butter

½ cup milk, heated

Salt and freshly ground pepper, preferably white pepper, to taste

1. Using a sharp boning or paring knife (not a vegetable peeler), pare off the skin and gnarly roots from the celery root. Rinse well. Cut the celery root into 1-inch chunks, paring away any soft woody spots. (The celery root can be stored in a bowl of cold water at room temperature for up to 8 hours. Drain well.)

2. Place the celery root and potatoes in a large saucepan and add enough lightly salted cold water to cover the potatoes by 1 inch. Cover and bring to a boil over high heat. Reduce the heat to medium-low and set the lid ajar. Cook until the potatoes are tender when pierced with the tip of a sharp knife, about 25 minutes.

3. Drain the celery root and potatoes well and return to the pot. Stir the vegetables over medium-low heat until they begin to film the bottom of the pot, about 2 minutes. Remove from the heat.

4. Add the butter to the potatoes. Using a potato masher or a handheld elec-

tric mixer, mash the potatoes, adding enough of the hot milk to reach the desired consistency. (The celery root mixture can also be puréed in a food processor. Don't try this with mashed potatoes alone—potatoes are too starchy and will turn into a gluey mess.) Season with the salt and pepper. Transfer to a serving dish and serve hot.

Brussels Sprout Chiffonade with Pancetta

Makes 8 servings

Make Ahead: The Brussels sprouts can be thinly sliced 1 day ahead, stored in plastic bags, and refrigerated. The pancetta can be prepared 2 hours before serving. The Brussels sprouts are best prepared just before serving.

Here is a fresh-tasting, quickly prepared recipe for Brussels sprouts, a vegetable that is often mishandled by overcooking. Thinly slicing the sprouts in a food processor will considerably reduce the cooking time, making them candidates for a fast sauté, flavored with pancetta, an Italian-style bacon that can be found at markets or delicatessens that carry Italian groceries.

Three 10-ounce containers Brussels sprouts, trimmed

3 ounces pancetta or bacon, sliced ⅛ inch thick

2 tablespoons olive oil

⅓ cup chopped shallots

¾ cup canned reduced-sodium chicken broth or turkey stock made from breast trimmings (see page 218)

Salt and freshly ground black pepper, to taste

1. Using a food processor fitted with the slicing blade, with the machine running, drop the Brussels sprouts through the feed tube to cut them into very thin slices. The slices do not have to be uniform. Just drop them through the tube (do not use the plunger to press them into the blade) and let them slice randomly. Or cut the Brussels sprouts crosswise by hand with a large, sharp knife. (The Brussels sprouts can be prepared, stored in plastic bags, and refrigerated for 1 day.)

2. Place the pancetta and oil in a Dutch oven or large saucepan. Cook over medium heat, turning the pancetta once, until the pancetta is crisp and brown, about 10 minutes. Using a slotted spatula, leaving the fat in the skillet, transfer the pancetta to paper towels to drain and cool. Coarsely chop the pancetta. (The pancetta can be prepared up to 2 hours ahead. Keep the pancetta and the fat in the skillet at room temperature.)

(continued)

3. Add the shallots to the pot and cook over medium heat, stirring occasionally, until softened, about 2 minutes. In batches, add the Brussels sprouts, letting the first batch wilt before adding another. Stir in the broth and cover. Cook just until the sprouts are tender, about 5 minutes. Stir in the reserved pancetta. Season with the salt and pepper. Serve hot.

Pumpkin Tart with Hazelnut Crust

Makes 8 servings

Make Ahead: The tart can be made up to 1 day ahead, cooled, covered, and refrigerated.

Pumpkin pie is so scrumptious that it shouldn't be reserved for holiday meals. This version is a very sophisticated rendition of the beloved classic. I have made pumpkin pie from scratch with fresh squash, but frankly canned pumpkin is very good and has the taste and texture that most people expect. For a professional-looking finish, fit a pastry bag with a ¹/₂-inch open star tip and fill with the whipped cream. Pipe whipped cream rosettes around the edge of the tart and sprinkle with chopped crystallized ginger.

Hazelnut Crust

¼ cup skinned and coarsely chopped hazelnuts (see page 235)

¼ cup confectioners' sugar

1 cup unbleached all-purpose flour

Pinch of salt

8 tablespoons (1 stick) unsalted butter, chilled and cut into 10 slices

1 large egg yolk

Filling

One 15-ounce can solid-pack pumpkin (1¾ cups)

¾ cup heavy cream

½ cup granulated sugar

⅓ cup packed light brown sugar (see Note, page 205)

1 large egg plus 2 large egg yolks, at room temperature, well beaten

1 teaspoon pumpkin pie spice or ½ teaspoon ground cinnamon and ¼ teaspoon *each* ground allspice and freshly grated nutmeg, and ⅛ teaspoon ground cloves

½ teaspoon ground ginger

Sweetened whipped cream (see Note), for serving

3 tablespoons finely chopped crystallized ginger, for garnish

1. Position a rack in the center of the oven and preheat to 375°F.

2. To make the crust, process the hazelnuts and confectioners' sugar in a food processor until the nuts are finely ground into a powder, about 30 seconds. Add the flour and salt, and pulse until combined. Add the butter and pulse until the mixture resembles coarse cornmeal with a few pea-sized chunks of butter. With

the machine running, add the yolk. Pulse just until the mixture begins to clump together. (If the dough is dry, add cold water, 1 teaspoon at a time, and pulse until moistened.) Gather up the dough.

3. Press the dough firmly and evenly into a 9¼-inch round tart pan with a removable bottom. Freeze for 15 minutes. Place the pan on a baking sheet.

4. To make the filling, combine the pumpkin, cream, granulated sugar, brown sugar, egg, yolks, pumpkin pie spice, and ginger in a medium bowl and whisk well to dissolve the sugar. Pour into the chilled crust.

5. Bake for 10 minutes. Reduce the temperature to 325°F, and continue baking until the filling is evenly puffed (the center may seem slightly uncooked), about 50 minutes.

6. Transfer to a wire cake rack and cool to room temperature. Remove the side of the pan. (The easiest way to do this is to place the pan on a large can, and let the side drop down like a ring around the can.) Serve the tart at room temperature (or cover loosely with plastic wrap and refrigerate until chilled), with a dollop of whipped cream and a sprinkle of chopped ginger.

Sweetened Whipped Cream

Place 1 cup chilled heavy cream in a chilled medium bowl, preferably stainless steel. Add 2 tablespoons confectioners' sugar and ½ teaspoon vanilla extract. Using a handheld electric mixer on high speed, whip the cream until it forms soft peaks. Cover and refrigerate until ready to serve, up to 8 hours. If the whipped cream separates during refrigeration, whisk or whip it until it thickens again.

An Intimate Thanksgiving Shopping List

Serves 8

Dairy

Unsalted butter (3 sticks)

Heavy cream (2½ cups)

Milk (½ cup)

Large eggs (4)

Delicatessen

Sliced pancetta, or sliced bacon (3 ounces)

Dried Herbs and Spices

Pumpkin pie spice (1 teaspoon or see substitutes in pumpkin tart recipe)

Ground ginger (½ teaspoon)

Groceries

Chicken broth, reduced-sodium (three 14½-ounce cans, plus ½ cup if not making quick turkey stock)

Dried cranberries (3 ounces)

Clam juice (two 8-ounce bottles)

Crystallized ginger (3 tablespoons, finely chopped)

Hazelnuts, preferably skinned (1 ounce)

Solid-pack pumpkin (one 15-ounce can)

Tomato paste (1½ tablespoons)

Liquor

Merlot (½ cup)

Dry sherry (½ cup)

Meat and Seafood

Fresh crabmeat (1 pound)

Turkey breasts (two 1½-pound boneless turkey breast roasts, or use one 5-pound whole breast, skinned and boned)

Pantry Staples

Hot red pepper sauce, as needed

Olive oil (2 tablespoons)

Cornstarch (½ teaspoon)

Unbleached flour (about 1⅓ cups)

Confectioners' sugar (6 tablespoons)

Granulated sugar (½ cup)

Light brown sugar (⅓ cup)

Vanilla extract (⅓ teaspoon)

Produce

Brussels sprouts (three 10-ounce containers)

Carrot (1 medium, if making quick turkey stock)

Celery (1 rib or 1 additional rib, if making quick turkey stock)

Celery root (3 pounds)

Yellow onions (1 large plus 1 small onion, if making quick turkey stock)

Parsley (1 bunch)

Baking potatoes (1 pound)

Rosemary (1 bunch)

Sage (1 bunch)

Shallots (2, for ⅓ cup chopped)

An Intimate Thanksgiving Preparation Timetable

1 day ahead

Make crab bisque; refrigerate

Roll turkey breasts; refrigerate

Make turkey stock; refrigerate

Cut Brussels sprouts into chiffonade; refrigerate in plastic bags

Make pumpkin tart; refrigerate

1 hour before serving

Roast turkey breasts

8 hours before serving

Prepare celery root and potatoes; store in cold water at room temperature

Make whipped cream; refrigerate

2 hours before serving

Cook pancetta; keep fat in pot

Just before serving

Make sauce for turkey breasts; slice breasts and serve

Cook Brussels sprout chiffonade

Make celery root purée

Cookie Swap

What is a cookie swap? Each guest brings a few dozen of their favorite holiday cookie in a container with a printed copy of the recipe. Some of the cookies are served at the party. The remainders are combined, and everyone goes home with a box full of assorted cookies and a collection of new recipes.

Diane's Nutty Thumbprints
Skip's Chocolate Bourbon Balls
Kelly's Sherry Cookies
Chris's Anise Cookies
Grandma Rodgers's Meringue Chip Cookies

It is not a competition, but an opportunity for friends and family to get together at a casual party during the busy holiday season.

There are a lot of great bakers in my immediate neighborhood—we're talking a few blocks in either direction. Some of them are professionals (Chris Styler is a cookbook author and has worked behind the scenes as kitchen manager on many television cooking shows; Kelly Volpe used to cook for The Grateful Dead; Diane Kniss once owned a bakery near Woodstock, New York, and is now my right hand in my kitchen), others are just passionate amateurs (Skip Dye works in publishing, but is one of the best cooks in town), and they all make a mean cookie.

A cookie swap is sugar-coated potluck, and this kind of party is heaven-sent to the host or hostess. I usually invite guests to arrive at 7:30 P.M., which should allow families with children to have an early dinner. This is meant to be a desserts-only affair, but if the majority of guests are coming directly from work, you may want to serve a selection of cold cuts to make sandwiches. Just keep any savory food on the simple side—there will be plenty of rich, heavy meals to come throughout the holiday season. Other than the cold-cuts option, the basic preparation for the party giver is easy: Bake a batch of cookies and brew a large pot of coffee. (Okay, you might have to clean up the house a little.) Guests also like cookie swaps because they can usually fit the cookie baking itself into their schedule a few days ahead of the actual party.

If you can, try to find out ahead of time what kind of cookie each person plans to make. You may want to steer someone away from making a chocolate chip cookie if you already have a couple of similar contributions. Considering the myriad cookies in the world, the law of averages would show that duplications would be rare, but keep an ear to the ground, just in case.

Perfect Cookies

After baking zillions of cookies over the years, I have a few basic tips to share. Set yourself up with the right equipment and you'll sidestep common frustrations.

Use heavy-gauge aluminum baking sheets Thin, flimsy cookie sheets translate into burned cookies. My favorite baking sheets, sometimes called half-sheet pans, are rimmed and measure about 17 × 12 inches.

Parchment paper is the cookie baker's best friend Parchment paper turns any cookie sheet into a nonstick pan. Even if a recipe doesn't call for a greased baking sheet, get in the habit of lining the sheet with parchment every time—you will only have to change the paper between batches, and skip the washing. Silicone baking pads, which can be used about a thousand times before replacing, are also great nonstick helpers.

When baking two sheets at the same time, switch the positions halfway through baking For the best results, bake the cookies one sheet at a time in the center of the oven, but most cooks like to speed things up and bake two sheets at a time. To ensure even baking, switch the positions of the racks from top to bottom and front to back halfway through baking. This is especially important in electric ovens with top-heating elements.

Let the baking sheets cool between batches If you put cookie dough on a warm baking sheet, the dough will melt and spread before it hits the oven. Not good. If the weather is cool, place the baking sheet near an open window to help it cool quickly. Don't run cold water over the baking sheets to speed things up, as you run the risk of warping them.

Buy airtight containers early in the season Old-fashioned cookie tins do a great job of keeping cookies fresh, but if you delay purchasing them, you could find yourself shut out. I have used new plastic storage containers (they come in many different sizes) instead with much success, but I have now marked my calendar to buy decorative containers in October.

Store each cookie in its own container Don't mix cookies because they can transfer flavors. Also, moist cookies can soften crisp cookies. If you combine cookies to make a gift assortment, separate the layers with wax paper.

Diane's Nutty Thumbprints

Makes about 3½ dozen

Make Ahead: The cookies can be made up to 3 days ahead, and stored in an airtight container at room temperature, or frozen for up to 2 months.

Diane Kniss has one of the most extensive and reliable collections of cookie recipes I've ever seen. Every year she and I get together and bake up boxes of cookies to give to our friends. We have a hard time deciding on each year's cookie bill of fare, but these wonderful treats, with their spicy, nutty filling, often make the final cut.

Cookie Dough

2½ cups all-purpose flour

½ teaspoon baking soda

¼ teaspoon salt

8 tablespoons (1 stick) unsalted butter, at room
    temperature, cut into pieces

1 cup packed light brown sugar (see Note, page 205)

1 large egg, at room temperature

1½ teaspoons vanilla extract

Filling

¾ cup (3 ounces) finely chopped pecans

⅓ cup packed light brown sugar

3 tablespoons sour cream

¾ teaspoon ground cinnamon

1. Position racks in the center and top third of the oven and preheat to 350°F.

2. To make the dough, sift the flour, baking soda, and salt together. Beat the butter and sugar in a large bowl with a handheld mixer on high speed until the mixture is light in color and texture, about 3 minutes. Beat in the egg, then the vanilla.

3. Roll the dough into 1-inch balls and place about 1 inch apart on ungreased baking sheets. Using your fingertip or the round end of a wooden spoon handle, make a ¼- to ½-inch wide indentation in the center of each cookie.

4. To make the filling, mix the pecans, brown sugar, sour cream, and cinnamon. Place in a sandwich-sized plastic bag and close. Snip off one corner of the bag

to make a ½-inch wide opening. (Or transfer the filling to a pastry bag fitted with a ½-inch wide plain pastry tip.) Squeeze the filling into the indentations.

5. Bake until the cookies are light golden brown, 12 to 15 minutes. Do not over-bake. Cool on the sheets for 3 minutes, then transfer to wire cooling racks to cool completely. (The cookies can be made up to 3 days and stored in an air-tight container at room temperature.)

Skip's Chocolate Bourbon Balls

Makes about 4 dozen
Make Ahead: The cookies must be made at least 1 day ahead, and can be stored in an airtight container at room temperature for up to 1 week.

Skip Dye hails from Tennessee, and when Christmas comes around, it's time for him to make his grandmother's recipe for a classic Southern holiday cookie, bourbon balls. These no-bake treats are often made with vanilla wafers, but this version uses chocolate-flavored graham crackers. The bourbon in the cookies needs to mellow before serving, so plan to make them at least a day ahead. Because the bourbon will preserve the cookies well, keep these in mind for when you need a make-ahead cookie. Don't freeze these cookies, as the sugar coating will dissolve.

1⅓ cups coarsely chopped pecans

1¼ cups confectioners' sugar

4 cups (13½ ounces) finely crushed chocolate-flavored graham crackers (crush in a plastic bag with a rolling pin or use a food processor)

½ cup unsweetened cocoa powder

4 tablespoons (½ stick) unsalted butter, well softened but not melted

¼ cup corn syrup

3 to 4 tablespoons bourbon

½ cup granulated sugar, for dipping

1. Process the pecans and ½ cup of the confectioners' sugar in a food processor until the nuts are finely ground. Transfer to a medium bowl and stir in the cookie crumbs. Sift in the remaining ¾ cup confectioners' sugar and the cocoa.

2. Add the butter and corn syrup. Add 3 tablespoons bourbon and mix with a rubber spatula, mashing the butter into the other ingredients. If the mixture is too dry and won't hold together, add the additional tablespoon of bourbon. Let stand until the liquid is absorbed, about 30 minutes.

3. Using a tablespoon for each, roll the mixture into balls. Roll the balls in the granulated sugar to coat. Let stand for 30 minutes or so, then roll again. Store in an airtight container and let stand at room temperature for at least 24 hours before serving. (The cookies can be made up to 2 weeks ahead. Roll the cookies in more granulated sugar before serving.)

Kelly's Sherry Cookies

Makes about 5 dozen cookies
Make Ahead: The cookies can be made 2 days ahead, and stored in an airtight container at room temperature, or frozen for up to 2 months.

Whenever Kelly Volpe makes these fragrant members of the thumbprint-cookie family, they bring back memories of her first childhood attempts at baking. She says that she always uses Harvey's Bristol Cream Sherry because that's what was in her family's liquor cabinet. Actually, any rich sherry on the sweet side, such as oloroso, is a good choice.

1 cup (2 sticks) unsalted butter, at room temperature

¾ cup sugar

2 large eggs, separated, at room temperature

¼ cup cream sherry

2½ cups all-purpose flour

1 cup (4 ounces) skinned and coarsely chopped skinned hazelnuts (see Note), or use walnut or pecan pieces

⅔ cup raspberry or apricot preserves, rubbed through a wire sieve

1. Position two racks in the center and top third of the oven and preheat to 350°F.

2. Cream the butter and sugar in a medium bowl with an electric mixer on high speed until the mixture is light in color and texture, about 3 minutes. One at a time, beat in the yolks, then the sherry. Using a wooden spoon, gradually stir in the flour.

3. Using a rounded teaspoon for each, roll the dough into 1-inch balls. Beat the egg whites in a small bowl. Place the chopped nuts in another bowl. One at a time, roll the balls in the whites, then in the nuts to coat. Place about 1 inch apart on ungreased baking sheets. Using your fingertip or the round end of a wooden spoon handle, make a ¼- to ½-inch wide indentation in the center of each cookie. Place the preserves in a sandwich-sized plastic bag and close. Snip off

one corner of the bag to make a ½-inch wide opening. (Or transfer the preserves to a pastry bag fitted with a ½-inch wide plain pastry tip.) Squeeze the preserves into the indentations.

4. Bake, switching the positions of the sheets from top to bottom and front to back halfway through baking, until the undersides of the cookies are golden brown (lift one up from the baking sheet to check), about 20 minutes. Cool on the sheets for 5 minutes, then transfer to wire cake racks to cool completely. (The cookies can be made up to 2 days ahead, and stored in an airtight container at room temperature.)

Note: Many supermarkets now sell skinned, chopped hazelnuts, which are a boon to busy bakers. If you have to skin the hazelnuts yourself, here's how to do it. Bake the hazelnuts in a preheated 350°F oven until the skins crack, about 10 minutes. Transfer the nuts to a clean kitchen towel. Wrap the nuts in the towel and let stand for 10 minutes. Use the towel to rub the skin from the nuts. Don't worry if you don't get every last bit of the brown skin off—a little bit will add color and flavor to your baking.

Chris's Anise Cookies

Makes 8 dozen cookies

Make Ahead: The cookies can be made up to 5 days ahead, and stored in an airtight container at room temperature, or frozen for up to 2 monhts.

You'll find these cookies on almost every Italian-American holiday table, and Chris Styler's family is no exception. Twisted into knots and sprinkled with candy confetti, they have a jaunty, festive look that really can perk up the cookie tray. This recipe makes a lot of cookies, which leaves plenty for gift giving, office parties, nibbling during tree trimming, and many other uses.

Cookies

4 large eggs

¾ cup vegetable oil

¾ cup granulated sugar

1½ teaspoons vanilla extract

4 cups all-purpose flour, as needed

2 tablespoons anise seeds

1 tablespoon baking powder

¼ teaspoon salt

Glaze

1½ cups confectioners' sugar

2 tablespoons anisette, rum, or water, as needed

Candy nonpareil confetti, for decorating

1. Position racks in the center and top third of the oven and preheat to 375°F.

2. To make the cookies, beat the eggs in a large bowl with an electric mixer on high speed until thickened. Gradually beat in the oil. Add the sugar in three additions, beating well after each addition. Beat in the vanilla. Using a wooden spoon, stir in 1 cup of the flour, anise seeds, baking powder, and salt. Stir in enough of the remaining flour to make a sticky, stiff dough.

3. Using a rounded teaspoon for each, roll the dough between your palms into a rope about ½ inch thick and 4 inches long. Cross each rope to make a loop (think of the commemorative ribbons people pin on lapels), and place about 1 inch apart on ungreased baking sheets. If the dough becomes too soft or sticky to handle, cover and refrigerate for about 30 minutes to chill slightly.

4. Bake, switching the positions of the sheets from top to bottom and front to back halfway through baking, until the cookies are light gold, about 10 minutes. Cool on the baking sheets for 3 minutes, then transfer to wire cake racks to cool completely.

5. To make the glaze, sift the confectioners' sugar into a small bowl. Add enough of the anisette to make a glaze with the consistency of heavy cream. One at a time, dip the cookies, rounded sides down, into the glaze and let the excess glaze drip back into the bowl. Lay the cookies on wax paper and sprinkle with the candy confetti while the glaze is still wet. Let stand to set the glaze. (The cookies can be made up to 5 days ahead, and stored in airtight containers at room temperature.)

Grandma Rodgers's Meringue Chip Cookies

Makes 3 dozen cookies

Make Ahead: The cookies can be made up to 3 days ahead, and stored in an airtight container at room temperature.

My grandmother called these "Surprise Cookies." The surprise must be that they don't contain any flour, making them a nice alternative to the typical holiday cookie. One piece of advice—if the weather is rainy or at all humid, don't make these cookies because the meringue just won't work. These cookies do not freeze well.

2 large egg whites, at room temperature

⅛ teaspoon cream of tartar

¾ cup granulated sugar

⅛ teaspoon salt

1 cup (6 ounces) semisweet chocolate chips

½ cup chopped walnuts

½ teaspoon vanilla extract

1. Position a rack in the center of the oven and preheat to 250°F. Line a baking sheet with parchment paper or wax paper. (Grandma used wax paper; I prefer parchment.)

2. Whip the egg whites and cream of tartar in a grease-free medium bowl with an electric mixer on high speed until the whites form soft peaks. One tablespoon at a time, beat in the sugar until the whites are stiff and shiny, then quickly beat in the salt. Fold in the chocolate chips, walnuts, and vanilla. Using a heaping teaspoon for each cookie, drop the meringue into mounds about 1 inch apart on the lined baking sheet.

3. Bake until the meringues are light gold and crisp, about 30 minutes. Cool completely on the baking sheet. If you have the time, let the meringues cool on the baking sheet in the turned-off oven with the oven door ajar. (The meringues can be made up to 2 days ahead, and stored in an airtight container at room temperature.)

Cookie Swap Grocery List and Preparation List

This party is different from the others, as the host or hostess will not be making all of the cookies. Use the recipe to make your shopping list of ingredients and plan the storage time for your chosen cookie.

A Christmas Eve Supper

For me, Christmas Eve was the most exciting night of the year because my brothers and I got to stay up so late. We had a pretty strange schedule for gift opening, which couldn't begin until after midnight on

---

Serves 12

Veal and Ricotta Lasagna

Italian Seafood Salad with Fennel and Olives

Romaine Antipasto Salad with Balsamic Vinaigrette

The Ultimate Garlic Bread

Pear Zuppa Inglese

Christmas Eve, a tradition that must have been brought over with Grandma Perry's family from Liechtenstein. As the years progressed, the rules were loosened to nine o'clock or so, but we still got home very late.

At Grandma's, we always had the same menu—sliced ham with plenty of fixings for sandwiches, her famous potato salad, and cookies. My own Christmas Eve dining requirements are different. We open only a few presents with close adult friends, and dinner is usually a sit-down affair. However, if kids attend, there are more presents, so the dinner plates get carried into the living room. In other words, I serve a menu that works both as a sit-down dinner and as a buffet meal.

The answer is lasagna, a make-ahead dish that has saved many a cook from last-minute hassles. I look for a hole in my cooking schedule anywhere before Christmas Eve, make the lasagna, and pop it in the freezer. With lasagna as the headliner, I keep the entire meal in the Italian vein—and why not? Everyone loves Italian food. Many Italian-American families serve only seafood dishes on Christmas Eve. I don't go that far, but seafood salad is an acknowledgment of this practice.

For a formal meal, serve the seafood salad first, then the lasagna with the salad on the side, and the bread throughout. For a buffet, serve everything together. No matter what configuration you end up with, a light red wine goes well with the menu. With eggnog as one of its main ingredients, the pear zuppa Inglese (Italian trifle) has "Christmas" written all over it. And if you have Christmas cookies, offer them as an extra gift to your guests.

Veal and Ricotta Lasagna

Makes 2 pans of lasagna; 9 servings each

Make Ahead: The lasagna can be made 1 day ahead or frozen for up to 1 month.

Tender chunks of veal make this lasagna extraordinary. Essentially, you are making a veal pot roast simmered in tomato sauce, which becomes the meat sauce for the lasagna. Even with "no boil" pasta, lasagna does take a bit of time, so keep in mind that you are getting quite a few servings for the investment. I make two pans, which ensures enough food for hearty appetites that may demand seconds and usually provides leftovers.

Veal-Tomato Sauce

3½ pounds boneless veal shoulder roast, rolled and tied (see Note)

¾ teaspoon salt

½ teaspoon freshly ground black pepper

4 tablespoons olive oil, divided

1 large onion, chopped

2 medium celery ribs with leaves, cut into ½-inch dice

4 garlic cloves, minced

Three 28-ounce cans crushed tomatoes with purée

1 cup dry white wine, such as Pinot Grigio or Sauvignon Blanc

2 teaspoons crumbled dried rosemary

2 teaspoons dried basil

Filling

Two 15-ounce containers part-skim or whole-milk ricotta cheese

8 large eggs, beaten

⅓ cup chopped fresh parsley

½ teaspoon salt

¼ teaspoon freshly ground black pepper

Two 9-ounce packages "no-boil" lasagna (see Notes)

6 cups (1½ pounds) shredded part-skim or whole-milk mozzarella cheese

½ cup (2 ounces) freshly grated Parmesan cheese

1. To make the veal-tomato sauce, season the veal with the salt and pepper. Heat 2 tablespoons of the oil in a large saucepan over medium-high heat. Add the veal to the saucepan and cook, turning occasionally, until lightly browned on all sides, about 8 minutes. Transfer the veal to a platter.

2. Heat the remaining 2 tablespoons oil in the saucepan and add the onions and celery. Cook until the vegetables are tender, about 8 minutes. Stir in the garlic and cook until the garlic is fragrant, about 1 minute. Stir in the tomatoes, wine, rosemary, and basil, and bring to a boil, stirring up the browned bits on the bottom of the pan. Return the veal to the pot. Reduce the heat to low and cover. Simmer until the veal is very tender, about 2½ hours. (The veal-tomato sauce can be prepared up to 1 day ahead, cooled, covered, and refrigerated.)

3. Transfer 3 cups of the meatless tomato sauce to a bowl and set aside. Transfer the veal to a carving board and let stand for 5 minutes. Remove the strings and cut the veal into ½- to ¾-inch pieces. Return the veal to the tomato sauce in the pot and mix well.

4. To make the filling, mix the ricotta, eggs, parsley, salt, and pepper in a medium bowl. Mix well.

5. Lightly oil two 13 × 9-inch baking pans. Spread 1 cup of the veal sauce in one pan. Place 3 lasagna strips, without overlapping the strips, in the pan (see Notes). Spread with about 1 cup of the ricotta mixture, then top with 1 cup veal sauce, and 1 cup mozzarella. Repeat with 3 lasagna strips, 1 cup ricotta, 1 cup veal sauce, and 1 cup mozzarella. Make another layer with the same ingredients. Top with 3 lasagna strips and 1½ cups of the reserved meatless tomato sauce. Sprinkle with half of the Parmesan. Cover with aluminum foil. Repeat with the remaining ingredients to make another pan of lasagna. (The lasagna can be prepared and refrigerated up to 1 day ahead. To freeze for up to 1 month, cover each pan with plastic wrap and then overwrap with aluminum foil. Remove the plastic wrap and replace the foil before baking.)

6. Position the racks in the center and top third of the oven and preheat to 375°F. Place each dish on a baking sheet or a large piece of aluminum foil. Bake the lasagnas for 35 minutes. Remove the foil and continue baking until

the sauce is bubbling throughout each pan, about 15 minutes. (If the lasagna has been refrigerated, allow an additional 10 minutes or so. To cook frozen lasagna, which should not be defrosted, bake for about 1 hour, 15 minutes; remove the foil and bake until bubbling, about 15 minutes.) Let stand 10 minutes before serving. Serve hot.

Notes: If you wish, 3½ pounds boneless veal stew, cut into 1-inch pieces, can be substituted for the veal roast. Brown the veal in batches in the oil in Step 1. In Step 3, use a slotted spoon to transfer the veal cubes and any clinging sauce to a food processor. Pulse the veal until it is coarsely chopped, and stir back into the tomato sauce in the pot.

Depending on the brand, "no-boil" lasagna may come in 8- or 9-ounce boxes. Some brands use 3 pasta strips per layer, and advise against overlapping the pasta. Therefore, adjust this recipe according to the specific directions on the box of the lasagna.

Italian Seafood Salad with Fennel and Olives

Makes 12 servings
Make Ahead: The salad can be made 1 day ahead, but is best served within 8 hours of making.

A classic of Italian cuisine, seafood salad is a sumptuous addition to a holiday buffet. It won't be the least expensive dish you've ever prepared, so be sure that you buy your seafood from a reputable fish market to avoid any disappointment on Christmas Eve. Nothing will ruin this salad more quickly than iodine-flavored shrimp. With the best ingredients, this is a splendid dish for a special holiday meal.

1½ pounds large (21 to 25 count) shrimp, peeled and deveined (see Note)

1¼ pounds bay scallops

¾ pound cleaned calamari, cut crosswise into ½-inch rings

1 large fennel bulb, fronds trimmed

¼ cup fresh lemon juice

½ teaspoon salt

¼ teaspoon crushed hot red pepper flakes

⅔ cup extra virgin olive oil

½ cup chopped pimento-stuffed green olives

3 tablespoons chopped fresh parsley, for garnish

1. Bring a large pot of lightly salted water to a boil. Add the shrimp and cook just until the shrimp turn pink, about 3 minutes (the water may not return to a boil). Using a large skimmer or small wire sieve, remove from the water and spread on a large baking sheet.

2. Return the water to a boil. Add the scallops and cook just until they turn opaque, about 1 minute or sometimes less. Remove from the water with the skimmer and transfer to the baking sheet with the shrimp.

3. Return the water to a boil. Add the calamari and cook just until they turn opaque, about 1 minute (sometimes less). Do not overcook. Drain in a colander. Add to the shellfish on the baking sheet and cool completely. When cool, cover tightly with plastic wrap and refrigerate until chilled, at least 1 and up to 8 hours. Drain the chilled seafood before using. *(continued)*

4. Cut the fennel in half lengthwise and trim away the hard core. Thinly slice the fennel bulb and stalks crosswise.

5. Place the lemon juice, salt, and hot red pepper flakes in a blender. With the machine running, add the oil.

6. Just before serving, mix the chilled seafood, fennel, and olives in a large bowl, and toss with the lemon dressing. Sprinkle with the parsley and serve chilled.

Note: Look for "easy-peel" shrimp, which really are easier to peel (they have been deveined, too). The shrimp may be medium instead of large, but that's no problem as long as you don't overcook them.

Romaine Antipasto Salad with Balsamic Vinaigrette

Makes 12 servings

Make Ahead: The vinaigrette can be made up to 1 day ahead. Make the salad just before serving.

Depending on whether you hit salami, cheese, red peppers, or artichoke hearts, this colorful salad offers up a different burst of savory flavor with every bite. The crisp, sturdy romaine leaves hold up well to the weight and texture of the other ingredients.

Balsamic Vinaigrette

¼ cup red wine vinegar

2 tablespoons balsamic vinegar

1 large garlic clove, crushed through a press

½ teaspoon salt

½ teaspoon freshly ground black pepper

1 cup extra virgin olive oil

2 large heads romaine lettuce, rinsed, dried, and torn into bite-sized pieces

Two 6½-ounce jars marinated artichoke hearts, drained and coarsely chopped

One 12-ounce jar roasted red peppers, drained and coarsely chopped (¾ cup)

8 ounces sliced salami, cut into ½-inch wide strips

1½ cups (6 ounces) shredded Provolone cheese

2 cups crisp bread croutons

1. To make the vinaigrette, combine the red and balsamic vinegars, garlic, salt, and pepper in a blender. With the machine running, gradually add the olive oil through the feed tube to make a smooth vinaigrette. (The vinaigrette can be prepared up to 4 hours ahead, and stored at room temperature. Blend again before using.)

2. Toss the lettuce, artichoke hearts, red peppers, and salami in a large serving bowl. Add the vinaigrette and toss again. Top with the cheese and croutons, and toss a final time. Serve immediately.

The Ultimate Garlic Bread

Makes 12 servings
Make Ahead: The bread can be made up to 8 hours ahead.

Garlic bread goes with so many buffet entrées that everyone needs a good recipe for this crowd-pleaser. My version uses dried basil (fresh basil turns black when baked and just isn't worth the expense here), fresh garlic and parsley, Parmesan cheese, and of course, plenty of butter.

8 tablespoons (1 stick) unsalted butter, at room temperature

2 large garlic cloves, crushed through a press

2 tablespoons chopped fresh parsley

2 teaspoons dried basil

¼ teaspoon freshly ground black pepper

1 long loaf crusty French or Italian bread, split lengthwise

½ cup (about 2 ounces) freshly grated Parmesan cheese

1. Mash the butter, garlic, parsley, basil, and pepper together in a small bowl until well combined. Spread evenly on the cut sides of the bread. (The bread can be prepared up to 8 hours ahead. Put the bread halves back together, wrap in aluminum foil, and store at room temperature. Separate the two halves of the bread and smooth the butter before proceeding.)

2. Position a broiler rack 6 to 8 inches from the source of heat and preheat the broiler.

3. Just before serving, sprinkle the buttered side of each bread half with ¼ cup Parmesan cheese. Broil the bread, cut side up, just until the cheese is melted and bubbling, about 1 minute. Transfer to a cutting board and cut crosswise into thick slices. Serve hot.

Herbed Turkey Breasts with
Cranberry-Merlot Sauce, page 216;
Celery Root Purée, page 219;
Brussels Sprout Chiffonade with
Pancetta, page 221

Pumpkin Tart with Hazelnut Crust, page 223

Italian Seafood Salad with Fennel and Olives, page 245

Veal and Ricotta Lasagna, page 242

Wine-Brined Pork Roast with Farmhouse Gravy, page 257

Orange Bûche de Noël,
page 262

Hot Crab and Artichoke Dip,
page 269; Spinach-Rice
Torta Squares, page 270;
Curried Glazed Peanuts,
page 272

Shrimp Spread with Pesto and Mascarpone, page 277; Mini-Meatballs in Chipotle Sauce, page 275; Cheese Straws with Feta and Sun-Dried Tomatoes, page 273

Pear Zuppa Inglese

Makes 12 servings

Make Ahead: The zuppa Inglese should be made at least 8 hours and up to 1 day ahead.

Zuppa Inglese ("English soup") has been a part of Italy's cuisine for centuries. It got its present name during the late nineteenth century, when British desserts became popular with the Italian upper classes. It does bear a resemblance to English trifle and like it, is one of the best holiday buffet desserts in the repertory. Instead of the customary custard sauce, use store-bought eggnog, which is very similar. You'll need a 3-quart trifle dish or a large glass bowl to hold the zuppa.

1 cup heavy cream

3 tablespoons confectioners' sugar

1 teaspoon vanilla extract

¾ cup canned pear nectar

¼ cup golden rum, optional, or use additional pear nectar

44 dry Italian ladyfingers (savoiardi), available at Italian delicatessens and many supermarkets

4 ripe Bartlett, Anjou, or Comice pears, peeled, cored, and cut into ¾-inch dice

½ pint fresh or frozen (individually frozen, not block) raspberries

3½ cups store-bought eggnog

⅔ cup (about 3 ounces) sliced almonds, toasted (see Note, page 103)

1. Start the zuppa Inglese at least 8 hours before serving. In a chilled medium bowl, whip the cream, confectioners' sugar, and vanilla with an electric mixer on high speed until the cream is stiff.

2. Mix the pear nectar and rum in a shallow bowl. One at a time, dip the ladyfingers into the pear nectar (do not soak) and stand them in a 3-quart trifle dish or glass bowl—you will need about 20 ladyfingers. Dip 8 more ladyfingers in the nectar, and break them up into the bowl. Top with half of the pears and raspberries, and 8 more dipped and broken ladyfingers. Slowly pour half of the eggnog over the pear-ladyfinger layer. Spread with half of the whipped cream

and sprinkle with ⅓ cup almonds. Repeat with the remaining pears and raspberries (reserve a few for garnish), ladyfingers, and eggnog. Spread with the remaining whipped cream. Sprinkle with the remaining almonds and garnish with reserved raspberries. Loosely cover the zuppa with plastic wrap and refrigerate for at least 8 hours, preferably overnight.

3. Serve chilled.

A Christmas Eve Supper Shopping List

Serves 12

Dairy

Unsalted butter (1 stick)

Eggnog (1 quart)

Mozzarella cheese (1½ pounds)

Parmesan cheese (4 ounces; buy freshly
grated, if you wish)

Provolone cheese (6 ounces)

Ricotta cheese (two 15-ounce containers)

Large eggs (8)

Dried Herbs and Spices

Dried basil (4 teaspoons)

Crushed hot red pepper flakes (¼ teaspoon)

Dried rosemary (2 teaspoons)

Groceries

Sliced almonds (about 3 ounces)

Marinated artichoke hearts (two 6½-ounce jars)

Bread croutons (2 cups)

Crushed tomatoes in purée (two 28-ounce
cans)

Crusty French or Italian bread (1 long loaf)

"No-boil" lasagna (two 8-ounce packages)

Italian-style ladyfingers, also called savoiardi
(two 7-ounce packages)

Pimento-stuffed olives (½ cup chopped)

Pear nectar (one 12-ounce can)

Roasted red peppers (one 12-ounce jar)

Liquor

Golden or dark rum (¼ cup)

Dry white wine, such as Pinot Grigio (1 cup)

Meat and Seafood

Cleaned calamari (¾ pound)

Bay scallops (1¼ pounds)

Large (21 to 25 count) shrimp (1½ pounds)

Boneless veal shoulder roast (3½ pounds)

Pantry Staples

Extra virgin olive oil (1⅔ cups)

Olive oil (4 tablespoons)

Balsamic vinegar (2 tablespoons)

Red wine vinegar (¼ cup)

Produce

Celery (2 ribs)

Fennel (1 bulb)

Garlic (1 head)

Lemons (2, for ¼ cup fresh juice)

Yellow onion (1 large)

Parsley (1 bunch)

Pears, such as Bartlett, Anjou, or Comice
(4 ripe)

Raspberries (½ pint fresh, or buy frozen
raspberries)

Romaine lettuce (2 large heads)

A Christmas Eve Supper Preparation Timetable

Up to 1 month ahead

Make lasagna; freeze

1 day ahead

Make zuppa Inglese; refrigerate

8 hours before serving

Make seafood salad; refrigerate

Make garlic bread; wrap, and store at room temperature

4 hours before serving

Assemble salad and make vinaigrette; refrigerate

About 2 hours before serving

Bake frozen lasagna (refrigerated lasagna only needs about 1 hour of baking)

Just before serving

Broil garlic bread

Toss salad

A Christmas Dinner

Even though I have many dinner parties during the year, none is more special than Christmas dinner. At other holidays, there may be a special centerpiece on the table to commemorate the occasion. But at Christmastime,

---

Serves 8

Smoked Trout Mousse and Toast Points on Baby Greens

Wine-Brined Pork Roast with Farmhouse Gravy

Potato and Cremini Mushroom Mash

Broccoli with Pine Nuts

Orange Bûche de Noël

---

the entire house is decorated, with the lights from the Christmas tree adding their sparkle to the dining room.

As for the dinner menu, the main course simply must be a roast, a tradition that harks back to ancient times. Meat was often slaughtered during the beginning of winter because the cold temperatures provided natural refrigeration. The best parts of the carcass were roasted and served for the holiday feast; the rest was salted or otherwise preserved.

While I find it hard to choose between main-course options

of roast beef, turkey, or pork, this wine-brined, roast pork shoulder has been such a hit with friends that I get annual requests for its repeat appearance. Brining, a technique that can add juiciness and flavor to meat and poultry, has many advocates. I wasn't a quick convert, mostly because finding room in a standard refrigerator for soaking the meat was a problem, and I didn't particularly like the salty flavor. However, with some adjustments, including the addition of wine, I've finally found a brine that I like.

There is always a lot of eating going on over the two-day Christmas holiday. If your family is like mine, you've hardly gotten over Christmas Eve's feast when you're expected to tuck into another full-scale meal. Keeping this in mind, be sure the first course is a light one—this mesclun salad with smoked trout mousse is ideal. Another couple of must-haves are mashed potatoes for the roast's gravy (here bolstered with lots of sautéed mushrooms) and a fresh green vegetable. To finish, a traditional dessert, such as orange bûche de Noël, is imperative. As wonderful as it is, I can't imagine serving it any other day of the year, and that is as it should be.

Smoked Trout Mousse and Toast Points with Baby Greens

Makes 8 servings

Make Ahead: The mousse can be prepared 2 days ahead, covered, and refrigerated. The vinaigrette can be prepared 4 hours ahead, kept at room temperature.

This is an elegant first course that would be nice with a glass of chilled champagne. Smoked trout used to be a bit difficult to find, but now I can get it at my local whole-sale price club and delicatessens. Some brands coat the trout with spices, which can be scraped off with a knife. If you wish, substitute smoked salmon for the trout. The lemon-shallot vinaigrette is thick and brightly colored, so take advantage of a fancy restaurant trick—drizzle it in an abstract pattern on the bare areas on the plate to create an edible garnish.

Smoked Trout Mousse

10 ounces skinless smoked trout fillet (see Note)

4 tablespoons unsalted butter, at room temperature

1 tablespoon fresh lemon juice

½ cup heavy cream

1 tablespoon chopped fresh chives

¼ teaspoon freshly ground black pepper

Lemon-Shallot Vinaigrette

Grated zest of 1 large lemon

⅓ cup fresh lemon juice

3 tablespoons chopped shallots

1 teaspoon Dijon mustard

½ teaspoon salt

½ teaspoon freshly ground black pepper

1 cup extra virgin olive oil

12 cups (about 11 ounces) mixed baby greens

8 slices firm white sandwich bread, toasted and cut into triangles

Chopped fresh chives, for garnish

1. To make the mousse, pulse the smoked trout in a food processor until chopped. With the machine running, add the butter through the feed tube, 1 tablespoon at a time, occasionally scraping down the sides of the bowl. With the machine running, gradually add the cream, and process until smooth. Add the chives and pepper, and pulse to combine. Transfer the mousse to a bowl, cover with plastic wrap, and refrigerate for at least 2 hours to blend the flavors. (The

mousse can be prepared up to 2 days ahead, covered, and refrigerated.) Remove the mousse from the refrigerator 30 to 60 minutes before serving to soften slightly.

2. To make the vinaigrette, combine the lemon zest and juice, shallots, mustard, salt, and pepper in a blender. With the blender running, gradually add the oil to make a smooth vinaigrette. (The vinaigrette can be prepared up to 4 hours ahead and kept at room temperature. Blend again until smooth before using.) Reserve 3 tablespoons of the vinaigrette for a garnish.

3. Just before serving, toss the greens and remaining vinaigrette in a large bowl. For each serving, use a soup spoon to scoop up a portion of the mousse. Using another soup spoon of the same size, mold the top of the mousse to make a smooth oval. Place the mousse on one side of a dinner plate. Use tongs to place a portion of the salad next to the mousse. Sprinkle the mousse and the bare part of the plate with the chives, then drizzle the reserved vinaigrette on the empty areas of the plate. Arrange 4 toast triangles on the plate. Serve immediately.

Note: If your delicatessen has whole smoked trout, ask the staff to fillet the trout for you. You will need 3 fillets from 1½ trout to equal 10 ounces. The delicatessen will probably ask you to buy both trout, of course. You can add the fourth fillet to the mousse if you wish, or flake the fillet and sprinkle it over each salad.

Wine-Brined Pork Roast with Farmhouse Gravy

Makes 10 to 12 servings

Although it isn't the most elegant cut, pork shoulder (often called picnic shoulder) has incredible flavor. It is best when cooked on the well-done side so the tough areas have time to tenderize and develop flavor. A typical 6-quart pot will hold a 9-pound pork shoulder for brining—if you want to brine a larger cut, you will have to improvise with a roasting pan or find a huge pot. While I use a slightly acidic, dry white like Sauvignon Blanc to make the brine and sauce, a heavier Chardonnay would be a better choice for serving with the roast.

Wine Brine

½ cup kosher salt or ⅓ cup iodized or plain salt

⅓ cup sugar

1 tablespoon dried thyme

1 tablespoon crumbled dried rosemary

1 teaspoon fennel seeds

1 teaspoon whole black peppercorns

2 bay leaves

One 750-ml bottle crisp, dry white wine, such as
    Sauvignon Blanc

One 9-pound fresh pork shoulder

1 cup crisp, dry white wine, such as Sauvignon Blanc or
    Pinot Grigio

1 cup canned reduced-sodium chicken broth

3 tablespoons unsalted butter

¼ cup all-purpose flour

Salt and freshly ground black pepper, to taste

1. To make the brine, combine 1 quart water with the salt, sugar, thyme, rosemary, fennel, peppercorns, and bay leaves in a large nonaluminum pot. Bring to a boil over high heat, stirring to dissolve the salt and sugar. Reduce the heat to low and simmer for 10 minutes. Remove from the heat and stir in the bottle of wine and 1 quart water. Cool completely.

2. Jab the skin of the pork shoulder all over with the tip of a small, sharp knife or sturdy meat fork, trying not to pierce the meat. (This helps promote crisp skin,

also called cracklings.) Otherwise, cut off and discard the skin, leaving a thin layer of fat on the meat. Submerge the pork in the cooled brine. Cover and refrigerate for at least 8 and up to 24 hours.

3.   Position a rack in the lower third of the oven and preheat to 400°F. Remove the pork from the brine and drain well. Place the pork, meatiest side up, on an oiled rack in a large roasting pan. Roast the pork for 15 minutes. Reduce the oven temperature to 325°F. Continue roasting until an instant-read thermometer, inserted into the center of the roast, reads 160°F, about 3 hours, 45 minutes longer, for a total roasting time of about 4 hours. Transfer the roast to a platter and let stand for at least 20 and up to 40 minutes before carving. Do not cover the roast—it will not cool too much.

4.   Meanwhile, pour the drippings out of the roasting pan into a 1-quart glass measuring cup, leaving all of the browned bits in the pan. Let the drippings stand for 5 minutes, then skim off and discard the fat that rises to the surface. Add the wine, broth, and enough cold water to the drippings to measure 3 cups.

5.   Place the roasting pan over medium heat on two stove burners. Add the butter and melt. Sprinkle in the flour, whisk until smooth, and let bubble for 1 minute. Whisk in the broth mixture and bring to a boil. Reduce the heat to low and simmer until lightly thickened and no trace of flour remains, about 5 minutes. Season carefully with salt and pepper—the brine-flavored drippings could have seasoned the gravy enough.

6.   Using a sharp knife, carve the roast, keeping in mind that pork shoulder has a complicated bone structure and that you won't get perfect slices. Serve immediately, with the gravy passed on the side.

Potato and Cremini Mushroom Mash

Makes about 10 servings
Make Ahead: The mushrooms can be prepared up to 4 hours ahead. The potatoes can be peeled and stored in a large bowl of cold water for up to 4 hours ahead. The mash is best made before serving.

British cooks call mashed potatoes "mash," which may not be the most appetizing word, but it is an appropriate name for this dish of creamy mashed potatoes combined with sautéed cremini mushrooms. If you wish, add 1 tablespoon of porcini powder to the mushrooms to give them an earthier flavor. To make porcini powder, just grind up an ounce or so of dried porcini mushrooms in a coffee grinder.

11 tablespoons (1 stick plus 3 tablespoons) unsalted
    butter, divided
1½ pounds cremini (baby portobello) mushrooms, thinly
    sliced
½ cup chopped shallots

5 pounds baking potatoes, such as russet or Burbank,
    peeled and cut into 2-inch chunks
Salt and freshly ground black pepper, to taste
⅔ cup heavy cream, heated until steaming hot, as
    needed
2 tablespoons chopped fresh parsley, for garnish

1. Melt 3 tablespoons of the butter in a large skillet over medium heat. Add half of the mushrooms and cook until they have reduced in volume to make room for the remaining mushrooms, about 5 minutes. Stir in the remaining mushrooms. Cook, uncovered, stirring occasionally, until all of the mushrooms are tender and the juices have evaporated, about 10 minutes. During the last 3 minutes, stir in the shallots. (If all of the mushrooms won't fit in the skillet, cook them in two batches.) Season with salt and pepper. (The mushrooms can be prepared up to 4 hours ahead and kept at room temperature. Reheat before adding to the potatoes.) Keep the mushrooms warm.

2. Meanwhile, place the potatoes in a large pot and add enough lightly salted cold water to cover the potatoes by 1 inch. Cover and bring to a boil over high

heat. Reduce the heat to medium-low and set the lid aslant. Cook until the potatoes are tender when pierced with the tip of a sharp knife, about 25 minutes.

3. Drain the potatoes well and return to the pot. To remove excess moisture and encourage fluffier potatoes, stir the potatoes over medium-low heat until they begin to film the bottom of the pot, about 2 minutes. Remove from the heat.

4. Add the remaining 8 tablespoons butter to the potatoes. Using a potato masher or a handheld electric mixer, mash the potatoes, adding enough of the hot cream to reach the desired consistency. Season with salt and pepper.

5. Stir about two-thirds of the mushrooms into the potatoes. Transfer to a serving dish and top with the remaining mushrooms. Sprinkle with the parsley and serve hot.

Broccoli with Pine Nuts

Makes 8 to 10 servings

Make Ahead: The blanched broccoli can be prepared, stored in plastic bags, and refrigerated up to 1 day ahead.

Even though it is now available year-round, I think of broccoli as a winter vegetable. Because it is so common, it needs dressing up to be appropriate for a holiday table. How about toasted pine nuts?

2 heads broccoli

½ cup (2 ounces) pine nuts

3 tablespoons unsalted butter

Salt and freshly ground black pepper, to taste

1. Cut the tops off the broccoli and cut into florets. Using a small, sharp knife, pare the thick skin from the broccoli stalks. Cut the stalks crosswise into ⅜-inch thick medallions.

2. To blanch the broccoli, bring a large pot of lightly salted water to a boil over high heat. Add the broccoli stalks and cook for 2 minutes. Add the florets and continue cooking until the broccoli is crisp-tender, about 3 minutes. Drain and rinse well under cold running water. (The broccoli can be prepared up to 1 day ahead. Wrap the broccoli in paper towels, store in plastic bags, and refrigerate.)

3. Heat a large, empty skillet over medium heat. Add the pine nuts and cook, stirring often, until lightly toasted, about 3 minutes. Transfer the nuts to a plate and set aside.

4. Melt the butter in the skillet over medium heat. Add the broccoli and ¼ cup water. Cook, stirring occasionally, until the broccoli is heated through and the liquid is almost evaporated, about 3 minutes. Stir in the pine nuts. Season with salt and pepper. Serve hot.

Orange Bûche de Noël

Makes 10 to 12 servings
Make Ahead: The cake can be made up to 1 day ahead.

One of my first catering jobs in New York was for a French diplomat, and, of course, bûche de Noël, the classic French holiday dessert, was de rigueur for the Christmas meal. Shaped like a Yule log, this impressive-looking cake is easier than the eight steps may suggest. (One secret is the use of marshmallow cream in the buttercream icing.) Use your imagination to garnish the cake—it should look as if it were in a woodland setting. Tucking clean pine boughs under the cake is a good start (be sure not to use any toxic plants such as holly or poinsettia), with store-bought chocolate truffles tucked between the branches. If you can find them at a candy shop or gourmet market, add chocolate twigs, meringue mushrooms, and marbleized candy "rocks."

Cake

3 tablespoons unsalted butter

1 teaspoon vanilla extract

6 large eggs, at room temperature

⅔ cup sugar

1 cup all-purpose flour

⅛ teaspoon salt

Confectioners' sugar, for sifting over the cake

Orange Buttercream Frosting

One 7-ounce jar marshamallow cream (1⅓ cups)

1 cup (2 sticks) unsalted butter, at cool room
    temperature, cut into 16 tablespoons

Grated zest of 1 large orange

6 tablespoons orange-flavored liqueur, preferably
    Grand Marnier (see Note)

¾ cup bitter orange marmalade

1. Position a rack in the center of the oven and preheat to 350°F. Lightly butter a 15 × 10 × 1-inch jelly-roll pan. Cut an 18 × 12-inch piece of wax or parchment paper. Cut a 2-inch long diagonal slit in each corner of the paper. Fit into the jelly-roll pan (the slits will help the paper make a smooth fit).

2. To make the cake, melt the butter in a small saucepan over medium heat. Pour into a medium bowl and stir in the vanilla. Set aside.

3. Crack the eggs into the bowl of a heavy-duty electric mixer or a stainless steel bowl. Whisk in the sugar. Place the bowl directly on a stove burner on very low heat. Whisk constantly just until the eggs are warm to the touch—the idea is to warm the eggs, not cook them. Remove from the heat. Using the whisk attachment (or a handheld mixer) on high speed, whip the eggs until they are very light and fluffy and have tripled in volume, about 4 minutes (allow 5 to 6 minutes for a handheld mixer).

4. Sift the flour and salt together. In two additions, sift the flour over the eggs, folding gently until the flour is almost but not completely incorporated. Add about 1 cup of the batter to the butter and fold together (this small amount of batter will deflate). Pour back into the larger amount of batter and fold together.

5. Spread the batter evenly in the prepared pan. Bake until the cake is golden brown and it springs back when pressed in the center, 15 to 20 minutes. Cool in the pan for 5 minutes. Sift the confectioners' sugar over the top of the cake. Place a clean kitchen towel and a flat baking sheet over the cake. Invert the cake, peel off the wax paper, and lay the paper back on the cake. Using the towel as an aid, roll up the cake into a cylinder (the wax paper will keep the cake from sticking to itself as it cools). Cool completely.

6. To make the frosting, place the marshmallow cream in a medium bowl. Using an electric mixer on high speed, beat in the butter, 1 tablespoon at a time. Beat in the orange zest.

7. Unroll the cake and discard the wax paper. Brush the liqueur evenly over the cake. Spread the cake with the marmalade. Roll the cake back up into a cylinder and transfer to an oblong platter. About 3 inches from one end of the cake, cut off a piece of cake at a sharp diagonal. Spread the cake with the frosting. Place the diagonal-cut slice on top of the cake to give a "stump" effect. Frost the "stump" along with the remaining cake. Draw the tines of a fork over the frosting to simulate bark.

(continued)

8. Refrigerate until the frosting is set, about 1 hour. (The cake can be prepared up to 1 day ahead, chilled, then covered loosely with plastic wrap.) Let the cake stand at room temperature for at least 30 minutes before serving to lose its chill.

Note: If you wish, substitute ⅓ cup fresh orange juice mixed with 2 tablespoons confectioners' sugar for the liqueur.

A Christmas Dinner Shopping List

Serves 8

Dairy

Unsalted butter (5¼ sticks)

Heavy cream (about 1 cup)

Large eggs (6)

Delicatessen

Skinless smoked trout fillets (10 ounces)

Dried Herbs and Spices

Bay leaves (2)

Fennel seeds (1 teaspoon)

Whole black peppercorns (1 teaspoon)

Dried rosemary (1 tablespoon)

Dried thyme (1 tablespoon)

Groceries

Sliced white sandwich bread (8 slices)

Chicken broth, reduced-sodium (1 cup)

Marshmallow cream (one 7-ounce jar)

Bitter orange marmalade (¾ cup)

Pine nuts (2 ounces)

Kosher salt (½ cup, or use ⅓ cup iodized salt)

Liquor

Grand Marnier or other orange-flavored liqueur
(6 tablespoons)

Dry white wine, such as Sauvignon Blanc
(2 cups)

Meat

One 9-lb fresh pork shoulder

Pantry Staples

Dijon mustard (1 teaspoon)

Extra virgin olive oil (1 cup)

Sugar (1 cup)

All-purpose flour (1¼ cups)

Vanilla extract (1 teaspoon)

Produce

Broccoli (2 heads)

Chives (1 bunch)

Lemons (3, for zest and 6 tablespoons fresh
lemon juice)

Mixed baby greens, also called mesclun
(11 ounces)

Cremini mushrooms, also called baby
portobellos (1½ pounds)

Parsley (1 bunch)

Baking potatoes (5 pounds)

Navel orange (1)

Shallots (5, for about ¾ cup chopped)

A Christmas Dinner Preparation Timetable

2 days ahead

Make the trout mousse; cover and refrigerate

1 day ahead

Brine and refrigerate pork

Trim broccoli; store in plastic bags and refrigerate

Make bûche de Noël; cover and refrigerate

About 4 hours before serving

Roast pork

Make lemon vinaigrette; store at room temperature

Sauté mushrooms for mash; store at room temperature

Peel potatoes; store in cold water at room temperature

1 hour before serving

Remove mousse from refrigerator and let stand at room temperature

Toast bread for salad

45 minutes before serving

Bring potatoes to a boil

Just before serving

Transfer pork to platter; make gravy

Make potato and mushroom mash

Toast pine nuts; cook broccoli with pine nuts

Remove bûche de Noël from refrigerator to lose chill

A Holiday Cocktail Party

New Year's Eve is the perfect time to indulge in the American tradition of the cocktail party. Of course, there are many times of the year when friends come together to lift a glass, but it is especially heartening to be

---

Serves 12

Hot Crab and Artichoke Dip

Spinach-Rice Torta Squares

Curried Glazed Peanuts

Cheese Straws with Feta and Sun-Dried Tomatoes

Shrimp Spread with Pesto and Mascarpone

Mini-Meatballs in Chipotle Sauce

Cherry-Chocolate Truffles

---

surrounded by close friends when toasting a happy new year.

Catered cocktail parties usually feature hors d'oeuvres passed on trays. But when the food is prepared by a lone cook, a different tactic is necessary because it is virtually impossible for one person to pass an assortment of individual hors d'oeuvres without serious help in the kitchen.

When I give a cocktail party, I rarely pass food because it takes me away from my guests. All that last-minute warming up and garnishing can really cramp a host's ability to socialize with his guests. Instead, I put out bowls and platters of food that allow the guests to serve themselves. Most of the recipes in this chapter are designed to be eaten as finger food. If you wish, put out small dishes and forks to facilitate the serving and eating of sauced items, such as the meatballs and shrimp.

It's important that there be a lot of food, because many guests will use the party as a substitute for a full-fledged dinner. You can supplement this menu with other recipes in the book that will work as finger food, such as the chicken wings or ribs (chopped with a cleaver into smaller pieces after grilling). Don't forget to put out a bowl to collect bones.

Just as it is helpful to streamline the food menu, it also helps to pare down the cocktail selection. In order to offer a full line of drinks, you must stock the bar and be prepared to know the formulas for a wide range of cocktails. Instead, choose one or two very special beverages. One year I poured martinis and Cosmopolitans, with Beaujolais Nouveau as an alternate for non-vodka drinkers; another year, an assortment of beers and ales. And, of course, champagne is always welcome at New Year's. But don't forget to have something interesting for the nondrinkers, such as sparkling apple cider or nonalcoholic eggnog.

Hot Crab and Artichoke Dip

Makes about 4 cups
Make Ahead: The dip can be prepared 1 day ahead.

Dips are the ultimate party food, and this hot dunk will disappear fast. The trick is how to keep it warm. Baked in a ceramic or glass round dish, it will keep warm for an hour or so—even when it's cold, people will still happily eat it. Or use a chafing dish (when was the last time you saw a recipe that used one of those?) or a small slow cooker.

1 cup mayonnaise

1 cup sour cream

1 cup (4 ounces) shredded extra-sharp Cheddar cheese

½ cup (2 ounces) freshly grated Parmesan cheese

1 garlic clove, crushed through a press

One 10-ounce box frozen artichoke hearts, thawed and chopped

12 ounces crabmeat, picked over for cartilage and shells

Hot red pepper sauce, to taste

Baguette Crisps (page 41), for serving

1. Position a rack in the top third of the oven and preheat to 400°F.
2. Mix the mayonnaise, sour cream, Cheddar and Parmesan cheeses, and garlic in a medium bowl. Stir in the artichokes and crab. Spread in a 1-quart round baking dish, a chafing dish, or the crockery insert of a small electric slow cooker. (The dip can be prepared up to 1 day ahead, covered, and refrigerated.)
3. Bake until the dip is bubbling, about 20 minutes, depending on the shape of the baking dish. If the dip is refrigerated, allow 30 minutes. Serve hot with the baguette slices.

Spinach-Rice Torta Squares

Makes 54 appetizers, 12 to 16 servings
Make Ahead: The torta can be made up to 1 day ahead.

There are many ways to vary these tasty bite-sized appetizers. You can substitute smoked mozzarella or feta cheese for the Cheddar, or sauté about $1/2$ cup of chopped prosciutto with the onions.

3 tablespoons packaged dried bread crumbs, preferably Italian-style

$2/3$ cup rice for risotto, such as Arborio

2 tablespoons olive oil

2 medium onions, chopped

2 garlic cloves, minced

Four 10-ounce boxes frozen chopped spinach, thawed and squeezed to remove excess liquid

12 large eggs

$1\frac{1}{2}$ teaspoons dried basil

$1\frac{1}{2}$ teaspoons crumbled dried rosemary

$1\frac{1}{4}$ teaspoons salt

$3/4$ teaspoon freshly ground black pepper

$1\frac{1}{2}$ cups (6 ounces) freshly grated Parmesan cheese, divided

1 cup (4 ounces) shredded smoked or extra-sharp Cheddar cheese

1. Position a rack in the center of the oven and preheat to 325°F. Lightly oil a 13 × 9-inch baking dish and sprinkle with the bread crumbs. Tilt the dish to coat with the crumbs, and tap out the excess.

2. Bring a medium saucepan of lightly salted water to a boil over high heat. Add the rice and reduce the heat to medium. Cook, uncovered, until the rice is tender, about 16 minutes. Drain well and set aside.

3. Heat the oil in a large nonstick skillet over medium heat and add the onions. Cook, stirring often, until the onions are tender, about 6 minutes. Add the garlic and stir until it gives off its aroma, about 1 minute. Add the spinach and cook, stirring often, just to evaporate any remaining liquid, about 3 minutes. Set aside.

4. Whisk the eggs, basil, rosemary, salt, and pepper in a large bowl. Add the rice, onions, spinach, 1 cup of the Parmesan, the Cheddar, and mix well. Spread in the baking dish. Sprinkle the top with the remaining ½ cup Parmesan. Bake until the torta feels firm when pressed in the center, about 45 minutes. Cool completely in the dish. (The torta can be prepared up to 1 day ahead, covered, and refrigerated.)

5. Cut the torta horizontally into 6 equal strips, then vertically into 9 strips to make 54 pieces. Arrange on a serving platter. Serve at room temperature.

Curried Glazed Peanuts

Makes 1 pound peanuts; 12 to 16 servings
Make Ahead: The peanuts can be made up to 3 days ahead.

My friend David Bonom is a recipe developer who creates delicious dishes for food magazines, and we are often on the phone swapping recipes. The first time I tasted his sweet-and-spicy peanuts, I thought they were the perfect cocktail nibble. Here is my version of this "bet you can't eat just one . . . handful" snack.

1 large egg white

1 pound unsalted roasted peanuts

⅓ cup superfine sugar (see Note)

3 tablespoons Madras-style curry powder

1 tablespoon sweet paprika, preferably Hungarian

2 teaspoons ground cumin

1 teaspoon garlic powder

1 teaspoon ground ginger

1 teaspoon salt, plus more to taste

1. Position a rack in the center of the oven and preheat to 325°F.

2. Whip the egg white and 1 tablespoon water in a medium bowl until very foamy. Add the peanuts and toss well to coat. Transfer to a colander. Shake well to leave a very thin coating of egg white on the peanuts.

3. Combine the sugar, curry powder, paprika, cumin, garlic powder, ginger, and salt in a medium bowl. Add the peanuts and mix well. Spread in a single layer on a large baking sheet.

4. Bake, occasionally stirring the nuts, until the spices are very fragrant and the coating has set (it will still seem slightly sticky), about 35 minutes. Cool for 10 minutes. Break the nuts apart as needed, then cool completely. (The nuts can be made up to 5 days ahead and stored in an airtight container at room temperature.)

Note: **If you don't have superfine sugar, just process ⅓ cup granulated sugar in a food processor or blender until the crystals are about half their original size.**

Cheese Straws with Feta and Sun-Dried Tomatoes

Makes 40 straws
Make Ahead: The straws can be prepared up to 2 days ahead.

I can't seem to give a cocktail party without making some kind of cheese straws, which are ridiculously simple to toss together with frozen puff pastry. Just about any sharp, semihard cheese will work—aged goat cheese, blue cheese, and Cheddar have all found themselves twisted between layers of puff pastry in my kitchen. Flavored feta cheese is available in a few different flavors, and the sun-dried tomato-and-herb version makes especially good cheese straws.

One 17¼-ounce package frozen puff pastry, thawed according to package directions

1 large egg white, beaten until foamy

2 cups (8 ounces) well-crumbled, flavored feta cheese, preferably sun-dried tomato-and-herb

1. Position the racks in the center and top third of the oven and preheat to 375°F. Line two large baking sheets with parchment paper or lightly butter them.
2. On a lightly floured work surface, unfold one pastry dough sheet, refrigerating the remaining pastry dough sheet. Dust lightly with flour and roll into a 14 × 10-inch rectangle. Brush lightly but thoroughly with the egg white. Cut the dough in half to make two 10 × 7-inch rectangles. Sprinkle half of the crumbled feta evenly over one of the rectangles. Top with the second rectangle, egg-white side down. Lightly roll the pin over the dough to make the cheese adhere between the layers of dough.
3. Starting on a long side, using a ruler and pizza wheel or a sharp knife, cut the dough into twenty ½-inch wide strips. Twist the strips into spirals and place ½ inch apart on the prepared (or nonstick) baking sheets, pressing the ends of the strips onto the sheets so the spirals won't untwist during baking. Repeat with the remaining dough, egg white, and cheese. Freeze the baking sheets for 10 minutes.

(continued)

4. Bake, switching the position of the sheets halfway through baking from top to bottom and front to back, until the straws are nicely browned, 20 to 25 minutes. Let cool for about 1 minute on the sheets, then transfer to wire cooling racks. Cool completely. (The straws can be prepared up to 1 day ahead and stored in an airtight container. Reheat and crisp in a preheated 350°F oven, uncovered, for 5 minutes.)

Mini-Meatballs in Chipotle Sauce

Makes 12 to 16 servings

Make Ahead: The meatballs can be prepared up to 2 days ahead, covered, and refrigerated, or frozen for up to 1 month.

For a filling warm hors d'oeuvre that doesn't need to be passed on a tray, meatballs are hard to beat. If you wish, serve a bowl of tortilla chips alongside, too, as the spicy sauce makes a pretty fine salsa.

3 tablespoons olive oil

2 large onions, finely chopped

4 garlic cloves, finely chopped

One 28-ounce can crushed tomatoes

One 15-ounce can tomato sauce

1 or 2 canned chipotles in adobo sauce (available at Latino markets and many supermarkets), finely chopped with any clinging sauce, to taste

¾ cup packaged dried bread crumbs

2 large eggs, beaten

1 tablespoon dried oregano

2 teaspoons salt

1½ pounds ground round (85 percent lean)

1½ pounds ground pork

½ teaspoon freshly ground black pepper

3 tablespoons chopped fresh cilantro, for garnish

1. Position a rack in the center of the oven and preheat to 400°F. Lightly oil a large baking sheet.

2. Heat the oil in a large saucepan over medium heat. Add the onions and cook, stirring often, until the onions are tender, about 6 minutes. Add the garlic and stir until it gives off its fragrance, about 1 minute. Transfer half of the onion mixture to a large bowl.

3. Return the saucepan with the remaining onion mixture to the stove. Add the tomatoes, tomato sauce, and chipotles, and bring to a boil. Cover and reduce the heat to medium-low. Simmer, stirring often, until the sauce is lightly thickened, about 30 minutes.

4. Meanwhile, add the bread crumbs, eggs, oregano, salt, and pepper to the onions in the bowl and mix well. Add the ground round and ground pork, and

mix again. Using about 1 tablespoon for each, roll the meat mixture into balls and place on the baking sheet.

5. Bake until the meatballs are browned, about 20 minutes. Transfer the meatballs to the simmering sauce. Cover and simmer until the meatballs are cooked through, about 15 minutes. (The meatballs can be prepared up to 2 days ahead. Cool the meatballs in the sauce. Cover tightly and refrigerate. Or transfer the cooled meatballs and sauce to airtight containers and freeze for up to 1 month; defrost before reheating. To reheat, cook the meatballs and sauce in a large saucepan over medium-low heat, covered, stirring occasionally, until the meatballs are heated through, about 20 minutes.)

6. Transfer the meatballs and sauce to a slow cooker or chafing dish to keep warm. Sprinkle with the cilantro. Serve hot with toothpicks for spearing the meatballs.

Shrimp Spread with Pesto and Mascarpone

Makes 12 to 16 servings

Make Ahead: The pesto can be made up to 5 days ahead. The dip can be assembled 4 hours before serving.

This three-toned spread is great slathered on anything crisp—baguette slices, crostini, bagel chips, flatbread, or even cucumber slices. Basil abounds in the summer, but most produce markets carry it year-round, so it can be used in winter menus, too. If you wish, instead of making the pesto, buy a ready-made version.

Pesto

2 cups packed fresh basil leaves

⅓ cup packed fresh parsley leaves, preferably flat-leafed parsley

¼ cup (1½ ounces) pine nuts or coarsely chopped walnuts

2 garlic cloves, crushed through a press

½ cup extra virgin olive oil, plus more for storing

½ cup (2 ounces) freshly grated Parmesan cheese

Salt and freshly ground black pepper, to taste

Two 8½-ounce containers mascarpone cheese, chilled

1½ pounds peeled cooked shrimp, tails discarded, meat coarsely chopped

Assorted crackers and crisp breads, for serving

1. To make the pesto, combine the basil, parsley, pine nuts, and garlic in a food processor or blender. With the machine running, slowly add the oil through the feed tube. (The pesto can be made to this point up to 5 days ahead. Transfer the pesto to a covered container, and float a thin layer of oil on top. Cover and refrigerate. Return to room temperature before proceeding.) Stir in the Parmesan. Season with salt and pepper.

2. Spread the mascarpone on a serving platter in a ½-inch thick layer. Spread the pesto on top of the mascarpone. Sprinkle the shrimp all over the spread. (The dip can be prepared up to 4 hours before serving, covered, and refrigerated.)

3. Serve chilled, with the crackers for spreading.

Cherry-Chocolate Truffles

Makes about 3 dozen truffles
Make Ahead: The truffles can be refrigerated for 1 week or frozen for up to 1 month.

When I was catering, chocolate truffles were my signature dessert. The wait staff would start passing them on silver trays about a half hour before the end of the party to signal politely that it might be a good time to get your coat. At a buffet, they can sit out in a cool place so people can serve themselves when they wish. In a warm room, the cocoa-rolled truffles may soften. To solve the problem, make the chocolate-dipped version, as the chocolate coating creates a hard shell to protect the filling from softening.

12 tablespoons (1½ sticks) unsalted butter, cut into pieces

1 pound bittersweet chocolate, finely chopped

½ cup cherry preserves, pulsed in a food processor to chop the fruit

¼ cup kirsch (cherry eau-de-vie, also called kirschwasser) or cherry brandy, or ¼ cup heavy cream

½ cup cocoa powder (preferably Dutch-processed such as Droste), for rolling

1. In a medium heatproof bowl set over a large saucepan of hot, not simmering, water, melt the butter. Add the chocolate and melt, stirring often, until smooth. Remove from the heat. Whisk in the preserves and kirsch. Cover loosely with plastic wrap and refrigerate until firm, at least 4 hours or overnight.

2. Place the cocoa in a shallow medium bowl. Line a baking sheet with aluminum foil. Using a melon baller, scoop the chilled chocolate mixture and roll between your palms to form a round truffle. (If the chocolate is too firm, let stand at room temperature to soften slightly.) Roll the truffle in the cocoa and place on the prepared baking sheet. Repeat with the remaining chocolate. (The truffles can be prepared up to 1 week ahead, stored in airtight containers, and refrigerated, or frozen for up to 2 months. Remove the truffles from the refrigerator 10 minutes before serving. Coat with additional cocoa, as needed.)

Chocolate-Dipped Truffles You will need an instant-read thermometer to check the temperature of the chocolate. After making the truffles, do not roll them in cocoa powder. Refrigerate the truffles on the foil-lined baking sheet while melting the chocolate. Place 12 ounces bittersweet chocolate, finely chopped, in the top part of a double boiler set over very hot, not boiling, water. Melt the chocolate, stirring often, until it is smooth and an instant-read thermometer inserted in the chocolate reads 115° to 120°F. Remove the insert from the pot and cool, stirring occasionally, until the chocolate is about 90°F. Place a dab of chocolate in the center of your palm. Pick up a truffle and roll it between your palms to coat with chocolate. Place on a foil-lined baking sheet. Repeat with the remaining truffles and chocolate. Refrigerate until the chocolate is set and the truffles release easily from the foil, about 30 minutes. Roll the coated truffles in cocoa powder.

A Holiday Cocktail Party Shopping List

Serves 12

Dairy

Unsalted butter (1½ sticks)

Large eggs (16)

Sour cream (1 cup)

Extra-sharp Cheddar cheese (4 ounces)

Smoked Cheddar cheese (4 ounces)

Feta cheese, preferably sun-dried tomato and
herb flavored (8 ounces)

Mascarpone cheese (two 8½-ounce containers)

Parmesan cheese (10 ounces; can buy freshly
grated cheese)

Dried Herbs and Spices

Dried basil (1½ teaspoons)

Ground cumin (2 teaspoons)

Madras-style curry powder (3 tablespoons)

Garlic powder (1 teaspoon)

Ground ginger (1 teaspoon)

Sweet paprika (1 tablespoon)

Dried oregano (1 tablespoon)

Dried rosemary (1½ teaspoons)

Frozen

Artichoke hearts (one 10-ounce box)

Chopped frozen spinach (four 10-ounce boxes)

Puff pastry (one 17¼-ounce box)

Groceries

Baguette-shaped French or Italian bread
(1 loaf)

Dried bread crumbs (about 1 cup)

Cherry preserves (½ cup)

Bittersweet chocolate (1 pound)

Dutch-processed cocoa powder (½ cup)

Crackers, for dip (as needed)

Mayonnaise (1 cup)

Peanuts, roasted unsalted (1 pound)

Pine nuts (1½ ounces)

Rice for risotto, such as Arborio (⅔ cup)

Crushed tomatoes (one 28-ounce can)

Tomato sauce (one 15-ounce can)

Tortilla chips (optional, as needed, for meatballs)

Chipotle chiles in adobo sauce (1 small can;
Latino groceries can be found at some
supermarkets)

Liquor

Kirsch or cherry brandy (¼ cup)

Meat and Seafood

Ground round (1½ pounds)

Ground pork (1½ pounds)

Crabmeat (12 ounces)

Shrimp, cooked and peeled (1½ pounds)

Pantry Staples

Hot red pepper sauce, as needed

Olive oil (5 tablespoons)

Extra virgin olive oil (½ cup)

Superfine sugar (⅓ cup, or use granulated
sugar)

Produce

Basil (1 large bunch, for 2 packed cups leaves)

Cilantro (1 bunch)

Garlic (1 head)

Parsley (1 bunch)

Yellow onions (2 medium and 2 large)

A Holiday Cocktail Party Preparation Timetable

1 month ahead

Make meatballs and sauce; freeze

Make cherry truffles; freeze

5 days ahead

Make pesto; refrigerate

3 days ahead

Make peanuts; store at room temperature

1 day ahead

Make crab dip; refrigerate

Make spinach torta; refrigerate

Thaw meatballs in refrigerator overnight

Make cheese straws; store at room temperature

8 hours ahead

Make baguette crisps; store in paper bag at room temperature

4 hours ahead

Make shrimp dip; refrigerate

Index

Quick Turkey Stock,
196–97
roasting times, 194
tips for a perfect turkey,
195

U
Utensils for cooking,
7–10

V
Veal and Ricotta Lasagna,
242–44
Vinaigrettes
Balsamic Vinaigrette, 247
Honey Vinaigrette, 145
Lemon-Shallot Vinaigrette,
255–56
Saffron Vinaigrette,
57–58
Tarragon Vinaigrette,
123
Toasted Pecan Vinaigrette,
17

Vodka
Jackie O's, 104
V-slicers, 8

W
Warming plates, 10
Watercress and Smoked
Salmon Sandwiches, 97
Whipped Cream,
Sweetened, 224
Wine
Cranberry-Merlot Sauce,
216–17
Kelly's Sherry Cookies,
234–35
Mimosa Sunrise, 113
Port Wine Syrup, 169
Red Wine Sauce, 72–73
Sherried Crab Bisque,
214–15
Sparkling White Sangria
Salad, 190–91
Wild Mushroom–Marsala
Sauce, 98–99
Wine-Brined Pork Roast

with Farmhouse Gravy,
257–58

Y
Yams/sweet potatoes
Mashed Honey-Roasted
Yams, 200
Sweet Potato King Cake,
47–48
Sweet Potato–Pineapple
Pie, 204–5
Yam and Yukon Gold
Potato Salad, 18–19
Yogurt-Chile Marinade, 55–56

Z
Zucchini
Cajun Ratatouille,
45–46
Fried Rice with Zucchini,
Corn, and Beans,
178–79
Zuppa Inglese, Pear,
249–50